Michael Farrell trained as
psychologist, and has s
education, management and consultancy.

In education he has taught both gifted and
profoundly handicapped children and worked as a
head teacher, the head of a unit in an internationally
renowned therapeutic community, and a lecturer in
special education at London University. He has
co-ordinated a national psychological project at City
University and currently directs a major education
project in London. As a consultant, he works on
personnel issues for international financial organizations and businesses. His interest in bereavement
stemmed from realizing how ill-prepared people are
for coping with the practical arrangements necessary
after a death. He has conducted seminars on
bereavement and is consulted by institutions working with bereaved children and adults.

Michael Farrell lives in Epsom, Surrey with his wife
and two daughters.

The Facts of Death

Coping When Someone Dies

MICHAEL FARRELL

ROBERT HALE · LONDON

© Michael Farrell 1991
First published in Great Britain 1991

ISBN 0 7090 4430 5

Robert Hale Limited
Clerkenwell House
Clerkenwell Green
London EC1R 0HT

Photoset in North Wales by
Derek Doyle & Associates, Mold, Clwyd.
Printed in Great Britain by
St Edmundsbury Press, Bury St Edmunds, Suffolk.
Bound by WBC Bookbinders Ltd, Bridgend, Glamorgan.

Contents

To my wife Marlyn and to our children
Anne and Sarah with all my love

Acknowledgements

I am grateful to many people who spoke to me or wrote about their experiences of bereavement while I was preparing this book.

Particular thanks are due to Richard Longhurst for commenting on the early drafts of part 1 and to David Chatterton for giving advice on part 2. Nicole Ray typed the manuscript with great efficiency. My wife gave unstinting encouragement and support throughout. I hope the book goes some way to repaying their generous help.

Preface

Facing Death

I have written this book to help you if you have to cope with the death of another person, probably a close relative.

In today's society, death tends to be a taboo subject and one which we find difficult to talk about or even contemplate. Yet most of us, probably all, at some time have to do our best to face the death of someone close to us.

You may care for someone through a long terminal illness. Professionals, family and friends may all add their support. But, when death eventually comes you are left feeling physically and emotionally drained.

Death may not be preceded by a long illness but may be sudden and unexpected. Here you are faced with the enormous shock of trying to deal with a situation for which you are unprepared. Another emotion often precipitated by unexpected death is guilt.

David, a baker, said this of his father's sudden death from a heart attack:

> I'd had a few cross words with him the day before he died and we hadn't really patched it up and got talking again. It wasn't about anything important, but when he died I kept going over it and over it in my mind. I kept wishing I could make it up to him but I couldn't. It was a long time before I could see that I was being too hard blaming myself. Everybody has rows sometimes and we were no different. I know and dad would have known that if he'd lived we would have laughed it off in no time.

Such guilty feelings are usually about regrettable things we have said or done, or about things we have left undone or unsaid. It often takes time, as David's experience shows, to see that such incidents are part of the pattern of everyone's life. Sudden death has taken away the opportunity to resolve the situation naturally. We usually have to try to resolve the situation within ourselves.

At such times, whether death was expected or not, we are often very vulnerable. You may know little or nothing about such things as the basic physical facts of death or what processes such as embalming involve. A natural fear of death may therefore be exacerbated by vague surmisings, by Job's comforters or by distorted tales heard second-hand and half remembered from the past.

The dictum, 'Where ignorance is bliss, 'tis folly to be wise' may hold true in some circumstances. But in the case of trying to cope with death and with bereavement, it is often easier to come to terms with the situation if you are aware of the plain facts. These can be less painful than what might be surmised.

Also, you may be understandably bewildered and confused when someone close to you dies. It is then harder to attempt to deal with the arrangements that need to be made. At such a time it may be helpful to know in outline what usually happens and to have practical guidance on such matters as funeral arrangements and dealing with the deceased's will.

This book aims to provide sufficient plain information about death and related topics to replace the vast amount of misinformation. Depending on individual circumstances, you may not need to read all the book and it has been set out in such a way that parts especially relevant to you can easily be found.

Several chapters in part 2 end with a listing headed 'Obtaining Current Figures'. This summarizes certain points dealt with in the particular chapter. For example, at the end of the chapter on 'Inheritance Tax', item 2 on the list is 'The limit of a small lifetime gift exempt from IHT'. Next to the circumstances is the amount given in the examples in the chapter. (In our instance this is £250). There is then a column for you to enter the current amount if it has changed. With minimum effort therefore you can ensure that your figures are up to date and your calculations accurate.

Addresses of organizations referred to in the text are listed at the end of the book.

Part 1

The Funeral and Related Matters

1   Expected and Peaceful Death

Signs of Death

When death has taken place, apart from signs like lack of
heart beat and absence of breathing, it is often noticeable
that the muscles of the deceased's face relax. This causes
the eyes to stare and the mouth to open. The skin loses its
usual tinge and becomes a rather waxen colour.

After death, the body loses heat and would be as cold as
the surrounding air temperature within twelve hours. The
blood begins to 'settle' in the body once the heart has
stopped pumping it round. Because of this, about three or
more hours after death, marks resembling bruises begin to
show on the back. (Assuming the deceased is lying flat on
his back.) The muscle stiffening known as rigor mortis
normally starts about six hours after death. Over the
following twelve hours, it affects the whole body. It then
fades away during the succeeding twelve hours.

Expected and Peaceful Death at Home

The deceased may die expectedly and peacefully in bed at
home. If so, it is not necessary to avoid touching anything
until the doctor is called for and arrives (as would be the
case if the death was unexpected).

You may wish to 'lay out' the deceased yourself.
Usually, however, 'laying out' is done by a member of the
funeral director's staff when someone has died at home.
The first person you need to contact is normally the doctor
and you will need to remember two main things.

17

First of all, find out if the doctor is going to come round to the house immediately. He may do so or he may arrange to see the body later. If he has been attending the deceased prior to death, he may not need to see the body at all.

Secondly, if the deceased is to be cremated, tell the doctor straight away. He then has to see the body, even if it is not immediately. He also has to contact a second doctor to look at the body.

In normal circumstances, the doctor who has previously been looking after the deceased will issue soon after the death a medical certificate of the cause of the death. The certificate is free. It is needed by the registrar of births, deaths and marriages so that the legal requirement can be complied with.

The certificate states the doctor's assessment of the cause or causes of death, the last date on which the doctor saw the deceased alive and whether or not the doctor has seen the body.

The doctor may send the certificate to the registrar of the area where the death occurred. Alternatively he may give it to you to take to the registrar, in which case it will be in a sealed envelope. The doctor will also give you a formal notice (notice to informant) which says that he has signed the medical certificate. The notice also tells you how to register the death and this has to be done in the district where the death happened.

If the dead person held a religious faith or subscribed to a system of beliefs, you might wish to contact the appropriate representative.

As well as contacting the doctor, you will need to contact a funeral director as soon as possible after death.

You may wish to ensure that any funeral director you consider using is a member of the National Association of Funeral Directors. If he is a member he has to abide by an established code of practice drafted in co-operation with the office of fair trading.

In the Yellow Pages directory, you will see some funeral directors with a display box entry showing the circular emblem of the association with the association's title written on the circumference and NAFD in the middle.

This does not mean that other Yellow Pages entries are not members but you would need to check with them.

Alternatively, the headquarters of the NAFD could give you the address and telephone number of local funeral directors who are members. It would be better to obtain this information sometime before the death takes place, if possible.

It is best to get two written estimates to compare prices. Having decided on a funeral director, your initial contact with him will probably be to ask for the laying out of the deceased to be performed. This is something that should be done as soon as possible.

The funeral director will need to know that the body is at home, rather than, for example, at a hospital. He will also need to know whether you want the body to be kept at home to await the funeral or whether you want him to remove the body to his own premises.

Even at this early stage, it would be best to make it clear to the funeral director if you do *not* wish the deceased to be embalmed. Some funeral directors embalm as a matter of course and some insist on embalming (unless the deceased has died of a blood-borne disease).

Returning to the laying out, where the body is removed from home before laying out is done, the funeral director will need instructions on two points.

First of all, say what you wish to be done with the clothing and any jewellery that the deceased may be wearing. Secondly, say how you want the body dressed, e.g. in a shroud, day clothes or night clothes.

If the deceased is not to remain at home, but is to be taken to the funeral director's premises, the body will be taken out in a sort of coffin or on a covered stretcher. It will then be transported in a plain van, an ambulance or a small hearse.

You will need to start the process of informing relatives and friends of the death. It might be possible to telephone five or six closest relatives and friends and ask them to contact others. This of course depends on individual relationships.

Where it is possible it takes away the extra pressure from you of making numerous telephone calls, or where people are not on the telephone, writing many letters.

Expected and peaceful death in hospital

Death may occur in a hospital when the next of kin are not present. Let us assume the deceased was an in-patient and the death was expected and peaceful.

In such circumstances, the ward nursing staff will contact you if you are the next of kin. The deceased may be laid out by a nurse and temporarily placed in the hospital mortuary.

Administrative staff working office hours usually deal with the formalities after a death. Because of this, if the deceased dies outside office hours, you will probably be given an appointment for the following day to sort out formalities. These will include collecting and signing out the deceased's belongings.

Normally, a hospital doctor will complete the medical certificate of the cause of death. If no hospital doctor has had the opportunity to assess the cause of death, then the deceased person's own doctor will be asked to issue the certificate. In most cases, should the certificate be issued by a hospital doctor, the body may be released to the family from the hospital mortuary pending the family signing a removal authority if there is one. But, procedures can vary from area to area. A medical certificate of the cause of death alone is not enough to allow removal in some cases. This can require removal authority, the completion of forms B and C and even registration. Once the body is ready to be released, you will need to contact a funeral director and the hospital may have a list of names, addresses and telephone numbers of local ones.

If you are a relative of the deceased or his executor, you will be able to sign a form (the removal authority) which is usually necessary to authorize the funeral director to take away the deceased.

If the deceased is to be cremated, the hospital will fill in the requisite forms. But make sure you tell them that cremation will take place. The doctor charges for this and the charge is usually added to the funeral director's bill.

When someone dies in hospital, an autopsy (post-mortem examination) may need to be conducted to find out more about the cause of death. If the next of kin agree to this they (or someone acting for them) will sign a consent form. A hospital arranged autopsy may lead to a slight delay in conducting the funeral.

Relatives may be asked permission for organs such as the eyes or heart of the deceased to be used for transplants. Even if the deceased has previously agreed to donate organs, say by completing a donor card, the hospital may still ask the relatives for their permission.

More information about the donating of organs and the body is given later.

2   The Registrar

To recap

Assume for the moment that one of two situations has arisen.

(a)   The deceased died expectedly and peacefully at home. The doctor has given you or has sent directly to the registrar the medical certificate of the cause of death. You have arranged the 'laying out' and may have had the body removed to the funeral director's premises.

You have made provisional arrangements for the treatment of the body and for the funeral with the funeral director. (This is explained in Chapter 5.)

(b)   The deceased died expectedly and peacefully in hospital (or in a similar establishment). The body has been laid out by a nurse and temporarily placed in the hospital mortuary. The medical certificate of the cause of the death has been issued by a hospital doctor (or in certain circumstances the deceased's doctor). The body has been released from the hospital mortuary. You have dealt with the formalities to have the body removed by the funeral director to his premises or perhaps to the deceased person's home. You have made provisional arrangements for the treatment of the body and for the funeral with the funeral director. (This will be explained later.)

We can now turn to the formalities of registering the death.

Who registers the death?

This depends on whether the death happened inside a building, such a house, or whether it occurred outside in the 'open air'.

If death took place in a building, the person who registers it (the 'informant') can be a relative who was with the deceased during his final illness or at death. Alternatively, the informant can be a relative living (or otherwise present) in the appropriate sub-district where the death has to be registered.

Where neither of these circumstances can be met, the informant can be anyone present at the death or the person who is to arrange the funeral.

If death occurred in a house, the occupier of the house or someone living in the house who knew of the death can act as informant. In an institution such as an old people's home, the senior resident officer can be the informant.

Who may register if death happens in the 'open air'? You can register the death if you are a relative and you have sufficient information about the deceased to satisfy the registrar. (The information the registrar will need is explained when we consider *how* death is registered.)

The informant may be any person present when the deceased died or anyone who found the body. The person making arrangements for the funeral can act as the informant.

You cannot register the death unless you 'qualify' in one of the above ways. The next of kin is generally the preferred informant all else being equal.

Where is the death registered?

Death must be registered at the offices of the Registrar of Births, Marriages and Deaths. It must be the office of the local sub-district where death took place (whether this was at home, in hospital or elsewhere) or where the body was found.

Your doctor's surgery, local library, local council, post office or police station will have the name, address and telephone number of the registrar. You should check that it is the correct registrar's office for your purposes and check their office hours. The address will also be in the telephone directory.

When should death be registered?

Death should be registered within five days.

Another nine days can be allowed if the registrar is given written confirmation that the doctor has signed the medical certificate of cause of death.

How is death registered?

To register the death, you will need to visit the registrar in his office hours. But, before considering what you need to do, we must return for a moment to the doctor who wrote the medical certificate of cause of death. The doctor also gives to the person who is to be the informant a notice to take to the registrar. The doctor may send the medical certificate of cause of death to the registrar. In this instance, the informant has to allow time for it to arrive before going to register the death. Alternatively, the doctor may give both the notice and the medical certificate of cause of death to the informant. In this case, if you are the informant, you will take both documents to the registrar.

If possible, take the deceased's birth certificate, marriage certificate and National Health Service medical card. These will help the registrar in recording the details he needs. If the deceased had a war pension order book, take that also.

The registrar will check that you 'qualify' as an informant and that the death occurred in his own sub-district. He will then fill in a draft form and will need the following information about the deceased:

- forename(s) and surname (and maiden name for a married woman)

- sex
- date and place of death
- date and place of birth (town and county, and country if born abroad)
- last 'home' address
- last full-time occupation
- whether retired
- the name and occupation of the spouse (if the deceased was married)
- in the case of a child under sixteen years old, the names and occupation(s) of parents
- marital status
- the date of birth of any widow or widower left
- whether the deceased was getting a pension or allowance from public funds

Once the draft form is completed, the entry is made in the register and the informant checks and signs it. The registrar next dates and signs the entry. He can then hand over the certificate of registration and the death certificate.

If it is necessary to apply for these from a registrar of another district, the local registrar will help you.

The certificates

(a) Certificate of registration of death (form BD8)

The certificate of registration of death will be given to you, free of charge, by the registrar once you have registered the death.

If for some reason the registration is held up, once the registrar has evidence of death, say from the doctor, he can give you the certificate of registration.

On the back of the certificate is a form which must be filled in if you are a widow and you need your retirement pension altered.

Also, use the certificate as evidence of registration of death when applying for any of the widow's benefits, money from the social fund to help pay for a funeral, or any other state benefits.

Further information about these state benefits is given

in a later chapter.

You send the form to your social security office.

(b) Death certificates

Apart from the certificate of registration of death, you will also need to get one or more of the death certificates described below.

There are several types of death certificates and you should, if possible, check which ones you will need before you see the registrar. A fee is payable.

The three main certificates and their purpose are as follows:

(i) Standard death certificate
   Purpose: to claim from private sources such as life insurance
   to claim from registered friendly societies
   to obtain probate
(ii) Special death certificate
   Purpose: to claim insurance taken out on the life of a parent or grandparent if you are the child or grandchild (or adopted/step child)
(iii) Certificate for certain statutory purposes
   Purpose: where probate is not required, for cashing National Savings certificates, premium savings bonds, and National Savings Bank deposits.

If the distinctions are not completely clear at the moment, they will become apparent once you have read the section of this book which concerns probate.

(c) Certificate for burial or cremation

In normal circumstances the registrar will give you the certificate for burial or cremation once you have registered the death. This is also known as the green form or the disposal certificate.

Take this certificate to the funeral director who then passes it on to the crematorium staff or church or cemetery staff depending on whether the deceased is to be cremated or buried.

Registering a still birth

A stillborn child is one born dead after the twenty-eighth week of pregnancy.

A certificate of still birth is given by the doctor if one attended the birth or by a certified midwife if she attended. If neither doctor nor midwife attended, a person qualified to be an informant can complete a form at the registrar stating that the child was stillborn (form 35).

The informant may be one of the following:

- the mother
- the father (if the child would have been 'legitimate' if it had been alive)
- the occupier of the premises where the still birth took place
- anyone present at the still birth
- anyone who found the stillborn child.

When the informant goes to the registrar, the registrar must have the certificate of still birth or the form completed by someone qualified to be an informant.

He will then need to know the following information about the mother:

- forename(s) and surname (and maiden name if married)
- place of birth
- usual residence at the time of the child's birth
- occupation
- whether never married

If the child would have been legitimate, had it lived, the registrar will need to know the father's forename(s), surname, occupation and place of birth.

If the father and mother are married to one another, the

registrar will ask the month and year of their marriage. He will also ask the number of any previous children born to the mother either by her husband or any previous husband. The number includes any stillborn children.

The registrar will then give you a certificate of burial or cremation and a certificate of registration of still birth.

If the baby's name is recorded in the register, the registrar will write the name on these certificates.

The health authority can offer to arrange a burial or cremation for a stillborn baby. It is free and it makes no difference whether the baby was born at home or in hospital.

The decision is normally made after discussion with the parent. If you accept, there would be a simple ceremony after which the baby would be buried or cremated.

You may be entitled to statutory maternity pay or maternity allowance. This may apply if the baby was stillborn within 11 weeks before the week in which it was expected. See leaflets FB8 entitled babies and benefits or NI 17A maternity benefits.

Registration and death abroad

Death may have taken place abroad, or on a foreign ship or aircraft. In such instances, you need to register the death in accordance with local requirements of the country concerned. You will require a death certificate from that country.

The death should also be registered with the British Consul so that a record of the death can be made in England. The death certificate can be later obtained from the consulate or the General Register Office.

Death may occur abroad under circumstances which, had it been in England or Wales, would have involved a coroner. If so, the death must be reported to the local coroner in the country concerned. (See also chapter 5, on section transporting the deceased over long distances.)

Registering death in Scotland

In Scotland, death is registered at the registration offices in the district where the deceased lived or where he died.

The informant may be one of the following:

- a relative of the deceased
- anyone present at the death
- the deceased's executor
- the occupier of the dwelling/premises where death occurred
- anyone who can give the registrar the necessary particulars

The particulars required by the registrar are similar to those required in England and Wales, plus the full names of any surviving spouse, time of death, whether the deceased's parents are still alive, their full names before marriage and the occupation of the deceased's father.

The registrar then issues a certificate of registration of death which you take to the funeral director. He passes it on to the appropriate authority, depending on whether the deceased is to be buried or cremated. Cremation and burial procedures are very similar to those of England and Wales except that local authority social work departments administer kirkyards. Death certificates other than the certificate of registration of death are similarly obtained to England and Wales. Death must be registered within eight days, a still birth within twenty-one days.

In the case of still birth, a doctor or midwife issues a certificate of still birth. Failing this, the informant completes a declaration form which he gets from the registrar. This form (form 7), must be completed and given to the registrar in order for him to register the death.

The procurator fiscal (see chapter 3) is informed by the registrar where it is necessary to use form 7 or when it is unclear whether the baby was dead at birth. He investigates and informs the registrar general.

Still birth is registered in the district where the mother normally lives or where the still birth occurred. Death must be registered before a cremation can be carried out, and this requires a certificate of still birth from the doctor who was present at the confinement, or who did the post-mortem.

3   The Coroner

Unusual death and the coroner

The deaths considered so far have been expected, peaceful deaths at home or in hospital. There were no complications and the registration of the death went ahead smoothly.

This is not always the case. As a form of shorthand, I am going to call all deaths other than the expected, peaceful deaths already considered, unusual.

Some unusual deaths may require the involvement of the coroner.

A coroner is a doctor or lawyer (or both) whose main job is to investigate any death reported to him. He is responsible only to the Crown and is independent of both central and local government.

Anybody can contact a coroner if they have misgivings about a supposed cause of death, but it is usually the doctor or the police who would do this.

Deaths which must be reported to the coroner

Here are some of the cases in which death has to be reported to a coroner:

1 The doctor did not treat the deceased during his final illness. (Doctor reports to coroner.)
2 The doctor did not see the deceased within fourteen days of the death. (Doctor reports to coroner.) Sometimes flexibility may be shown in this matter if all

the parties (family, doctor and coroner's office) agree.
3 Death was sudden and unexplained.
4 Death was attributable to an 'industrial' disease.
5 In certain circumstances, when the death was caused, or contributed to, by an injury sustained on military service.
6 Death happened in suspicious circumstances.
7 Death was owing to an accident or injury. The accident or injury may have occurred some considerable time before death, perhaps a year or more. If it is possible that death was related to the accident or injury, the coroner will still take an interest.
8 Death was by suicide.
9 Death *may* be owing to poisoning, neglect, drug dependence, drug abuse or abortion.
10 Death occurred before a patient had recovered from anaesthesia.
12 Death occurred during a surgical operation.
13 Where there was some doubt about whether the child was alive after birth.

When there is an unusual death

You may be present at a death or discover a body where death may eventually need investigating by a coroner. For example, death might be owing to an accident.

In such a situation, call the police immediately either by contacting the local police station, or by dialing 999 for the emergency services and asking for the police.

Do not move or touch anything at the scene of the death; the police will want to examine the area first. They may, for instance, need to take away with them anything that could relate to the cause of death. Such items would constitute evidence if there was a coroner's inquest.

The police will probably ask for a statement if you were present at the death or discovered the body. If there is a coroner's inquest later you may be required as a witness.

The coroner can call witnesses, whether or not they have made a police statement, if he considers that they can give pertinent information.

You may find a body or be present at a death which does not appear to need a coroner's involvement, but which is still not an expected, peaceful death at home. In this case, call the doctor immediately. Do not move the body unless essential. Avoid touching or moving anything until the doctor arrives. One reason for this is that he may decide it is necessary to inform the police. They in turn may involve the coroner.

I have mentioned that anyone with reasonable cause may contact the coroner. The local police station will help you get in touch with, or pass your information on to, the coroner's officer (usually a policeman).

This more direct course of contact with the coroner might be appropriate, for example, if you think that a relative had died partly as a result of an industrial injury which may have been sustained in the past and may be unknown to his present doctor.

Circumstances may dictate that you should also contact the deceased person's nearest relative or the local representative of his religious faith.

If you have any doubt at all that the person is dead, then dial 999 for the emergency services and request an ambulance.

How you may be informed of an unusual death

A person may die unexpectedly or may be involved in an accident and taken to hospital where he dies. In these cases, the next of kin may be traced and informed by the police rather than by hospital staff.

Where the deceased was not an in-patient in the hospital concerned, a family member may be asked to visit the hospital to identify the body.

If it is necessary for the death to be referred to the coroner, the responsibility for the body is assumed by the coroner's office and not the hospital. The hospital will tell you how to get in touch with the coroner's office who will provide information.

How deaths are normally referred to a coroner

Normally, the coroner is contacted by a doctor or the police. The doctor will usually contact the coroner direct before death is registered.

The registrar may receive a medical certificate of the cause of death from a doctor and decide it is necessary to inform the coroner. If the coroner decides that the cause of death is natural, he tells the registrar to accept the medical certificate. The death can then be registered by the informant.

The registrar will let the informant know (providing he has the address and telephone number). If the death was reported directly to the coroner, the informant has to contact the coroner's office to get clearance to visit the registrar.

On the other hand, the coroner may consider that the death needs investigating. This delays formalities because the registrar cannot register the death until a clearance is received from the coroner.

An interim certificate of death can be obtained from the coroner which will normally be sufficient to allow you to begin dealing with the deceased's estate.

In some of the cases which the coroner investigates, he will order a post-mortem examination. This is usually to determine the cause of death. The consent of relatives is not needed for this. You can, however, choose a doctor to be present. The coroner will pay for the removal of the body from the place of death to the mortuary for post-mortem examination. You may choose which funeral director is involved.

Should the examination show that death was from natural causes, the coroner may issue a notification called a pink form (form 100). This gives the cause of death. The coroner may give this form to you to deliver to the registrar, or he may send it to the registrar directly. Death is then registered in the normal way.

The funeral can now progress. Indeed, you may have made all the provisional arrangements with the funeral director while waiting for the body to be released.

To establish when the body is to be released by the

coroner, check with his office if it is their custom to inform the next of kin when this takes place. If it is not you will need to check with them every couple of days. As soon as they tell you that they have sent the registrar notice of their findings, go to the registrar and register the death.

If the deceased is to be buried, the registrar will issue a green form. You take this to the funeral director.

If the deceased is to be cremated, it is the coroner who issues the certificate for cremation (form E). Collect the certificate from the coroner's office or arrange for the funeral director to collect it as soon as it is ready. Death can then be registered.

The funeral director will collect the deceased from the mortuary where the body will have been kept under refrigeration. The funeral director can then take the deceased to the funeral parlour.

The coroner's inquest

A coroner's inquest will be held if the death was violent and unnatural or caused by an industrial disease. An inquest is also necessary if, after an autopsy, the cause of death remains uncertain.

The inquest seeks to establish, among other things, the identity of the deceased, how, where and when he died, and the 'category' of his death (for example suicide or unlawful killing).

A date for the inquest is decided and the procedure takes place in a coroner's court which is a special court of law.

The coroner may have written statements from various people who know about the death. He may have transcripts of interviews (carried out by the police) with others who have evidence. Where witnesses are required to attend the court personally they will receive a summons.

Each witness is called to the witness box by the coroner and is sworn in. The coroner then asks him questions. If the coroner agrees, the witness can then be questioned by other people attending the inquest who have an accepted interest in the case. These might be the spouse or the parents or children of the deceased. Others might include a representative of the company who insured the deceased. People with an 'interest' in the case may be represented by a lawyer. You may only ask questions about the medical cause and circumstances of the death.

Once the coroner has heard all the evidence he gives his findings.

In England and Wales the record of the findings is called a statement of inquisition while in Northern Ireland it is known as a verdict.

The findings comprise the following:

1 The deceased's name, if known.
2 The verdict on the cause of death.
3 The disease or injury which caused death.
4 The time, place and circumstances of any injury which was sustained.
5 Where and when the deceased died, deceased's full name, sex, age (or likely age), profession or rank, and address. This information is sent to the registrar of births, deaths and marriages).

The verdict on the cause of death is one of the following:

> Killed unlawfully
> Killed lawfully
> Execution of a death sentence
> Suicide
> Abortion
> Accident or misadventure
> Industrial accident
> Open verdict
> Natural causes
> Want of attention at birth
> Dependence on drugs/abuse of drugs
> Industrial disease

In the case of the last four causes, the coroner may add that the cause of death was aggravated by lack of care or self neglect.

In the case of suicide, the coroner may add that the deceased took their own life while the balance of their mind was disturbed.

In Northern Ireland, the verdict comprises the following information all of which is sent to the registrar:

1 Deceased's full name
2 Sex of the deceased
3 Date of death
4 Place of death
5 The deceased's usual address if this was not the place of death
6 Marital status
7 Date and place of birth
8 Occupation
9 Maiden name
10 Cause of death
11 Findings

For the findings the coroner writes a statement concerning how death occurred. Sometimes, the inquest requires a jury to decide the verdict.

Between seven and eleven men and women eligible for jury service are summoned, just as they would be for a case in the crown court. Having heard all the evidence, and having been guided on points of law by the coroner, the jury decide the verdict. If they cannot reach a unanimous decision, a majority verdict is acceptable.

Once a verdict is reached, whether by the coroner alone or by a jury, the coroner is able to send the necessary information to the registrar to enable the death to be registered.

Sometimes, a coroner has to adjourn an inquest, say when someone has been charged with causing the death. In such cases the coroner can give an interim certificate to the next of kin or executors of the deceased. This enables you to start claiming benefits and begin dealing with the deceased's estate.

If the inquest has to be adjourned, the coroner sends the registrar the information needed for death to be registered five days later.

Once the registrar has the information he needs, he himself registers the death. It makes no difference whether the information was provided after a verdict or an adjournment. There is no need to visit the registrar as an informant. You can collect the death certificate from the registrar once he has registered the death.

In all cases, when there has been an inquest, the coroner issues a certificate authorizing either burial or cremation according to the wishes of the next of kin. These are either an order for burial (form 101) or a certificate for cremation (form E). A leaflet 'The Work of the Coroner – a Home Office Guide' printed by HMSO in 1984, might be found useful.

When an inquest is necessary there may well be delays in conducting the funeral.

Scotland – the procurator fiscal and the public inquiry

In Scotland, a law officer under the authority of the Lord Advocate and known as the procurator fiscal assumes the duties of the English coroner.

A death may be reported to the procurator fiscal by the registrar if a medical certificate of cause of death cannot be supplied. Also, the procurator fiscal can ask a doctor to give a second opinion on the cause of death, if not satisfied with the initial medical certificate.

Should the procurator fiscal deem a post-mortem necessary, permission is sought from the sheriff.

As in England and Wales, an inquest is sometimes called, so in Scotland certain circumstances require a public inquiry. If the procurator fiscal thinks that the cause of death needs looking into further, he first talks to relatives and any others present at the death. He informs the Crown Office and the Lord Advocate, and then decides whether to ask the sheriff for a public inquiry to be held in the sheriff's court.

At any such inquiry, the procurator fiscal examines witnesses and informs the Registrar General of the findings. He in turn passes the information to the appropriate local registrar who registers the death or alters any existing registration accordingly.

4 Donated Body or Organs

When the body is donated

The deceased may have bequeathed her or his body for anatomical purposes. A medical school could then use it for research or for medical examination.

The procedures and rights of relatives are determined by law. The deceased may have talked over with you his wishes concerning the donation of his body. He may have prepared for this by writing to the London Anatomy Office.

He would have requested a form which would have been completed and kept with the will and other papers. In any event, when the person dies, you need to act quickly. Get in touch with Her Majesty's Inspector of Anatomy. The inspector keeps up to date with the needs of all the medical schools in the country. .

If the death is in Scotland or Northern Ireland, you should telephone the nearest medical school.

It is important to remember that a body will not always be accepted by a medical school. Possible reasons for rejection are the following:

1 The donor lived a long way from the medical school.
2 Death came soon after an operation.
3 The death is being investigated by a coroner.
4 A post-mortem examination has already been conducted.

Let us assume that the body is accepted.

The medical school will arrange for the body to be collected by a funeral director. They will send you forms to complete and return.

You will need to get a medical certificate of the cause of death from your doctor. Next, register the death and get the certificate of burial or cremation. This disposal certificate should be sent to the medical school.

Tell the medical school whether the deceased wished to be buried or cremated and they will normally comply with this.

The body may be kept for teaching purposes for up to 2 years. But the medical school can let relatives know when the body is available for a funeral.

If everything is left to the medical school, they will pay for a simple funeral including a service said by a minister of the appropriate faith. They will cremate the body or bury it but will not arrange memorials such as a headstone.

Should any arrangements more elaborate than these be required, you would have to pay for the extras, even if the medical school agreed to them.

The deceased's relatives can override his bequest of his body. Relatives are legally entitled to determine how the body should be disposed of.

When organs are donated

The deceased may have agreed to donate an organ or organs by signing a donor card. He will have probably mentioned this to you if you are next of kin. The organs may be the heart, lungs, liver, kidneys, eyes, pituitary gland or pancreas.

As soon as the doctor has certified death, ask him (if he is your GP) to notify the local hospital or contact them yourself.

If the body is not already in hospital, it will be taken there for an operation to remove the organ(s) concerned. They are handed on to a doctor or another staff member of the transplant service.

The body may then be collected (by, for instance, the funeral director) and arrangements for the funeral can carry on as normal.

When the corneas of the eyes are donated, these are usually removed by a specially trained person within twelve hours of death. This can be done at home, in hospital or at the premises of the funeral director. Let your doctor know the situation and contact the nearest eye hospital urgently.

If the deceased has died suddenly in hospital, say following a road accident, the staff may ask the next of kin if they would consent to an organ or organs being used for transplant.

Although this is obviously a time of great shock, some people feel that they can give permission. They may say afterwards that they were glad that they did so, giving the chance of life or of a fuller life to someone else. But this is a personal decision.

If the deceased had particularly asked that his body should *not* be used for medical purposes, these wishes will be respected.

If the deceased has not made his views known then organs may be donated providing relatives do not object.

On the other hand, if the deceased has made it clear that he wishes to donate organs, relatives have no right in law to prevent this. In practice, doctors use discretion if relatives object.

Should the death have been reported to a coroner, his permission must be obtained before organs can be donated.

The British Organ Donor Society (BODY) is a self-help support group for families of organ donors and for those who have received organs.

They can be telephoned between 9.30 a.m. and 3 p.m. on weekdays. Outside these times there is a 24 hour answerphone.

5   The Funeral Director

People often feel a certain uneasiness when considering the quality of service in funeral arrangements. It is as though you feel you might be dishonouring the dead by worrying about such market slogans as 'value for money' and 'quality of service'.

Yet it should be remembered that funeral directors run a business. One of the purposes of that business, like any other, is to make money. It is quite proper that we should have certain expectations when entering into the business transaction.

Of course this is not to deny that at his best the funeral director offers practical help and support at a crucial time.

The code of practice

I mentioned earlier about the probable initial contact with the funeral director. This might have been to arrange the laying out of the deceased, to remove the body to the funeral director's premises or to have the body embalmed.

It might be worth ensuring that the funeral director is a member of the National Association of Funeral Directors. Assuming that the chosen funeral director is a member he should abide by a code of practice as follows:

1 To observe the confidence of every client at all times.
2 At all times to render good service and make fair charges in respect of services rendered and for merchandise supplied.
3 To ensure that advertising is always in good taste. No

sensational, offensive or undignified advertising is permitted.

4 To provide clients with full and fair information about services. Price lists or leaflets covering the basic simple funeral and all types of coffins, caskets and services provided should be readily available to clients.

5 To give a written estimate of all funeral charges and disbursements to be made on a client's behalf in each and every case at the time of taking instructions, or, failing this, as soon as it's practicable before the day of the funeral.

6 To provide all clients with itemized accounts.

7 Never to conduct themselves at any time in a manner likely to prejudice their profession. The soliciting of funerals or the offering or giving of any reward for recommendation is not permitted.

8 To display on premises the association symbol to publicize observance of the code of practice. Members may also display this code of practice statement.

9 The National Association of Funeral Directors sponsors the code and provides a clients' advisory service with conciliation and arbitration arrangements available to help resolve any dispute which may arise between members and their clients.

Embalming

Let us briefly reconsider what services the funeral director may so far have performed.

He may have collected the deceased from home, hospital mortuary or elsewhere and removed the body to the funeral parlour. He may have laid out the body and provided a robe to dress it.

He may have embalmed the body. This cannot be done, however, until the medical certificate of cause of death has been issued. If there is to be cremation, two doctors must have completed the requisite forms. When a coroner has been involved, he has to give authority before embalming is done.

What exactly is embalming and what is involved? It is

carried out partly to temporarily preserve the body and partly for cosmetic reasons. Because the process replaces body fluids which may have been lost in a long illness, for example, it fills out the body and face to their usual proportions and restores natural skin colour.

Embalming is usually done in a special preparation room at the funeral director's premises. A preserving fluid is injected under pressure into an artery and as the fluid enters the body, the blood is allowed out at another point through a vein. Stomach contents are cleaned out by inserting a trocar into the stomach. This is a long hollow needle inside a tube.

If the deceased is a woman, the embalmer may use make-up on her face. Embalming is by no means essential, and if you do not want it done, tell the funeral director at the earliest opportunity.

Some funeral directors who may not embalm keep the deceased in refrigerated compartments in order to help preserve them.

The type of funeral

Once the formalities of having the death registered have been completed and you have the certificate of burial or cremation (the green form) firm arrangements may be made for the funeral. Provisional arrangements can be made before you have the disposal certificate. But this certificate is needed before you can go ahead with certainty.

You may visit the funeral director at his premises or arrange for him to see you at your home. You will have told the funeral director earlier whether burial or cremation is planned and he will contact the appropriate authorities to arrange this. Because this procedure differs for burial and cremation, I will describe it in a later chapter.

The main decision now concerns the type of funeral and the cost of it. This relates to the type of coffin chosen. An expensive coffin comes with an expensive funeral, while a plainer coffin means a simple funeral. The funeral director will usually show a series of pictures of the various coffins from which a choice can be made.

It is helpful to discuss with family and others beforehand to decide what extras might be needed. These might include extra cars following the hearse, notices in the newspapers and so on. When considering notices, specify amongst other things if the funeral is private and whether flowers are *not* to be sent. If flowers are to be sent, say where.

Once the requirements are decided, the funeral director should be able to give a written estimate. Ask him to itemize all his services including, if relevant, such things as laying out, removing the body to his premises and embalming.

Also, he should be able to list and include in his estimate charges which he has to pass on for costs outside his control. These may include crematorium or cemetery fees, doctor's certificates and clergy fees. The funeral director has to pay VAT on services provided to him, which he must pass on to you. His own services do not attract VAT.

Notice that item 4 of the NAFD code of practice refers to a basic simple funeral. This is the least expensive funeral and is arranged for an overall price. An itemized breakdown of such a funeral is not given. It includes a coffin and hearse with a following car. (The distance the cars travel is limited and further distances outside the standard would be charged extra.) Bearers for carrying the coffin and the services of the funeral director are included. Any extras to the basic funeral are charged for. So it is worthwhile making sure what the particular funeral director does and does not include in this basic price.

A basic simple funeral would not for instance cover such things as church or crematorium fees, notices in the local paper or flowers.

Deciding on the form of ceremony

This section concentrates on the practicalities of deciding a form of ceremony appropriate to the wishes and beliefs of the deceased.

The funeral director can help arrange the service or ceremony and you will have to decide several things. First of all, where will the ceremony take place? It may be in a chapel at the funeral parlour if there is one. The venue may be a place of worship appropriate to the deceased's faith. A cemetery chapel may be used or the service may be held in the cemetery itself or in a churchyard. If the deceased is to be cremated, the crematorium chapel is often used.

Next, consider who will officiate. In the case of a church service this would be the clergyman. Where the ceremony is non-religious an officiant with experience in leading such a ceremony would be appropriate.

Whoever the officiant, you or the funeral director will need to contact them and confirm that they can attend. The availability of the venue and that of the officiant will help you fix the date and time of the ceremony.

It will be necessary to know the proposed duration of the ceremony. Restrictions may be placed on this for example where another service is to be held soon after at the same venue. Get the funeral director to check all this.

The form of the ceremony for a religious service will be to an established pattern or order of service. Decide on any music or readings, taking into account any wishes the deceased may have expressed.

If the ceremony is non-religious, its structure should be made clear to everyone. The officiant might briefly explain the order of the ceremony at the beginning or there may be printed copies for mourners.

It may be intended to hold a non-religious ceremony, or no ceremony at all, or a ceremony of another denomination.

If so and if burial is to be in a churchyard, then the parish incumbent should be given 48 hours written notice.

Where a cemetery or crematorium are to be involved, they should be similarly informed.

Transporting the deceased over long distances

The funeral director will make arrangements if it is necessary to transport the deceased over long distances, including assisting in the completion of necessary forms.

It may be that the deceased dies while visiting another part of the country. Depending on the distance, the body may be brought home by hearse, rail or even by air. All of these means can be very expensive, particularly air transportation, so the funeral director should advise of all the charges involved.

Sometimes the funeral director may have to call on the services of a colleague in that part of the country where the death occurred. For example, the colleague may be asked to embalm the body before transportation as well as arranging the removal of the deceased from his premises. Where this is necessary, your contract remains with the 'home' funeral director who passes on his contracted out costs to you.

Even longer distances may be involved. The deceased may have to be transported abroad. Perhaps he was resident abroad and had expressed a wish to be buried there and was visiting home when he died.

If a body is to be moved out of England and Wales, the coroner has to give permission. This permission has to be obtained at least four days before the body is to be moved. The time period is at the coroner's discretion and is to enable him to carry out any necessary enquiries.

You will then receive a removal notice (form 104), part of which has to be sent to the registrar.

If the death occurred abroad, you can arrange for a local burial or funeral. The British Consul in the country concerned can register the death. A record of it will be kept at the General Register Office in London.

If death takes place abroad and you want to bring the body back to England and Wales you will need a death certificate from the country in question. Alternatively, you may get an authorization from the coroner or similar authority to remove the body from the country.

To arrange a funeral in England or Wales when death has occurred abroad, you need two documents:

1 An authenticated translation of the foreign death certificate (or a death certificate issued in Scotland or Northern Ireland).

2 A certificate of no liability to register. This is obtained from the registrar in England and Wales for the relevant sub-district where you wish to bury or cremate the body.

If you wish to arrange a cremation in England and Wales in these circumstances, you also require a consent form from the Home Office. This is in a sense in place of the forms B and C which are normally completed in England and Wales by two doctors.

An application form (form A, application for cremation) has to be filled in by the deceased's next of kin or executor.

A death certificate is needed from the country in which the deceased died and which shows the cause of death. These two documents in an envelope marked 'cremation urgent' have to be sent to the Home Office.

If death has occurred abroad and the deceased has been transported to England or Wales, the coroner in England or Wales may still need to take an interest in the death.

Procedures for Scotland are rather different. When a body is to be moved out of Scotland for cremation and burial in another country, you must first register the death in Scotland. Cremated remains can be taken out of Scotland without formality. If the body is transported from Scotland to England or Wales for burial, the 'receiving' registrar will want a standard death certificate or a certificate of registration from you. If the body is brought from abroad, the registrar in Scotland does not require evidence that the death occurred elsewhere. Should the body be coming from England or Wales, a coroner's form which gives permission for the body to be removed must be given to the person responsible for arranging the place of burial or cremation. If the body is brought to Scotland for cremation, apply to the Scottish Home and Health Department who will get permission for the cremation to take place under the authority of the Secretary of State for Scotland. You will need the foreign death certificate. If you have cremated remains brought into Scotland, they must be accompanied by the certificate of cremation from the foreign crematorium.

Viewing the deceased

Usually, the deceased is kept at the funeral parlour, although sometimes the body is kept at home and placed in a church on the night before the funeral service.

If the body is at the funeral parlour, you may wish to view the deceased. If the body is to be embalmed, it is viewed after this has been done. Should the funeral director not embalm, the body would be stored in refrigerated unit.

Let the funeral director know when you wish to view the deceased. Before your arrival, the body will be placed in a special private room, usually called a chapel of rest.

Many people have expressed views on whether it is better to view the deceased or not. When viewing is possible it can help the bereaved's awareness of the reality of death. Where cosmetic work by the funeral director has been able to minimize the effect of disease or an accident, viewing can help modify previous images of the deceased's last days and provide a more acceptable one for the memory of the bereaved.

Yet each of us is different. Although the reasons just given for viewing the deceased sound compelling, they are not. Some people do not have to view to accept the reality of death. Some can remember clearly happier times when the deceased was vigorous and healthy as well as the last days of his life when he may have been physically affected by illness.

So try to feel no pressure either way. None can say for others that it is better to view the deceased or not. You have to decide for yourself.

Paying for the funeral

The cost of the funeral is normally met from the deceased's estate.

The funeral director should send a detailed account showing a breakdown of items and services which he has provided directly and those which he has paid for on your behalf. The latter, where appropriate, should be accompanied by receipts. Confirm that where value added tax is payable, it is calculated and itemized.

If there are any complaints about the bill or the service that the funeral director has provided or omitted, tell him first and try to have matters put straight.

Should you still not be satisfied, try the citizens advice bureau or a trading standards department.

If they cannot resolve the problem, contact the National Association of Funeral Directors.

If still not satisfied, pay a fee to use arbitration. An independent arbitrator will decide the issue and his decision will be binding on you and the funeral director. The arbitration fee is returned if the finding is in your favour.

As an alternative to arbitration, you could, after seeking advice, take the case to court.

6   Burial or Cremation?

Burial

If the deceased is to be buried, you will have informed the funeral director at the earliest opportunity and he will have made the necessary preliminary arrangements.

Let the funeral director know whether it is proposed to have the deceased buried in a churchyard (or its adjoining cemetery), local authority cemetery or private cemetery.

Should you wish a churchyard or church cemetery to be used, the funeral director will confirm with the incumbent of the church that this is possible.

If there are members of the deceased's family or relatives of the deceased buried in the churchyard/cemetery, the deceased has a right to burial there. So does anyone who died in the parish, providing of course there is room. If the deceased's permanent address was in the parish, he is also entitled to burial in the churchyard/cemetery.

Otherwise, the funeral director will apply on your behalf to the incumbent and parochial church council, and will be bound by their decision.

If you wish to apply for the sole use of a particular plot, the funeral director will apply to the diocesan registrar for a faculty. This is a licence reserving a grave plot but it does not transfer ownership of the land from the church to you.

Unless the deceased or someone in the family has made this application, two months before the deceased's death, faculty burial is impracticable as the application takes about six weeks to process.

This does not prevent someone applying for a faculty on

the grave plot allocated by the church incumbent in order to reserve it for other family members who die in the future.

Presuming that the application for burial proceeds satisfactorily, the funeral director will arrange and confirm a suitable time for the burial.

The funeral director will pay fees to the church, that is to the incumbent, officials and council, according to what is required.

Fees are paid for the following:

- the church service preceding burial
- burial
- the grave digger
- any music such as the organ
- extra heating in the church

For faculty graves you also pay as follows:

- a faculty fee
- a fee for having a headstone removed and replaced on an existing grave when a subsequent body is buried
- an internment fee to the church incumbent for each burial in a family grave

You may not be able to secure a burial plot in a churchyard or church cemetery. However, the funeral director may know a local cemetery, perhaps run by the local authority or a private company, which has part of its ground consecrated to the Anglican church. If he arranges burial there, the funeral director will pay the clergyman for carrying out a service when there has been no church service immediately before.

A local authority or private cemetery may have part of its ground allocated to members of other denominations. While most such cemeteries are non-denominational, they usually allow a religious service of any denomination, a secular service, or burial without any form of ceremony. This should also apply to their chapel if they have one.

The funeral director should know the regulations of

such cemeteries and their fees. He should also know exactly what you get for the fee. Check with him such things as whether memorials are permitted and possible charges for maintaining the grave.

The next of kin or executor may be asked by the funeral director to sign an application form for a burial in a local authority cemetery. He will ensure that necessary documents are sent to the cemetery on time.

Having sent the application form for burial to the cemetery superintendent, the funeral director will confirm it is accepted, arrange the time of the burial and order the type of grave required. He will also apply for the grave deeds to the burial authorities.

After burial, these authorities send the executor or next of kin a copy of the entry in the burial register. The register is a record of ownership of the plot and of any previous burials there.

Types of graves

The cost of a grave depends on its size as well as its type. The least expensive is one with no right to exclusive burial. The cemetery may arrange not to bury anyone else in the plot for a certain number of years, but you may have to pay a fee for this arrangement.

Another type of grave is one giving the right to exclusive burial. There will probably be a time limit of say fifty years on this right. Should you wish, this sort of grave can be a lawn grave. This means that only a simple headstone can be erected while the rest of the grave plot must be left to grass. Such a grave is less expensive than one with extra fittings because it is easier and cheaper to maintain.

For a private grave a deed of grant is required for which you may have to pay. What happens after the first burial has been made and the grave is to be used for a subsequent burial? The deed of grant must be provided which the owner of the grave plot has to sign before the grave can be reopened. An additional interment fee has to be paid and a fee for the removal and replacement of the headstone.

Any grave with no right to exclusive burial is always simply dug out of the earth. But for graves with exclusive burial rights, the grave can be lined with brick at an extra cost. Making the arrangements for this and having the grave built can take several weeks.

A vault is simply a grave that is completely lined with brick. It can also be a bricked double grave.

The day of the funeral

Assume that the time of the burial, and any service which may be planned, has been confirmed. You will then be able to fix the time for the start of the funeral, and inform mourners accordingly of all funeral details.

Usually, this will begin where the body is (at the funeral parlour or at home). Or the body may be taken to the church or cemetery and the mourners meet there. The coffin may be taken to the church the evening before the funeral and placed in front of the altar to await the service the following day.

Where the body is at the funeral parlour, and there is a chapel on the premises, you may wish to hold a service there before proceeding to the burial site.

Should flowers have been requested, these are placed on the coffin in the hearse. If the funeral director is arranging cars for family and others, he will arrange that the cortège is formed at a particular time.

For a church service prior to burial, bearers take the coffin from the hearse and into the church where it is placed in front of the altar. When the service is over, the bearers take the coffin from the church to the grave site preceded by a member of staff connected with the burial site.

If there is no service, the coffin is taken from the hearse and straight to the grave site. The same procedure follows if the service had been held somewhere else, such as the funeral parlour or at a church some distance from the burial site.

At the graveside, the bearers place webbing slings

underneath the coffin and lower it into the grave. The words of commital are said as the coffin descends. The mourners usually then leave the graveside.

After the funeral, you may have arranged for mourners to take a little food and drink at the home of a close relative of the deceased or at a local restaurant.

Go through all these details with the funeral director and let him know exactly what he should do.

The estimated bill should reflected all the services requested.

The monumental mason

Should you want some kind of memorial or headstone erected in the cemetery or churchyard, contact a local monumental mason.

The firm of funeral directors may be linked with a monumental mason. If not, write to the National Association of Master Masons for the address of a local firm.

The firm should be able to advise about any restrictions that the cemetery authorities or the church authorities place on the nature of the proposed memorial.

They should also be able to apply to the appropriate authority for permission to erect a memorial and establish the fees involved.

Make sure all these details are checked and any permission necessary is received in writing before confirming your order for a memorial.

Also, get a detailed estimate from the mason of the total cost of the memorial (including the cost of having it erected) and the fees the mason will pay on your behalf to church or cemetery authorities.

Cremation

Forms to be completed

Once the funeral director is told that the deceased is to be cremated, he should arrange for various forms to be completed. He should have a stock of these.

Forms A, B, C, E and F and others may be involved depending on the circumstances. Form A is the application for cremation which is filled in by next of kin or executor.

Another form, not given an alphabetical label, has to be completed to specify how the ashes are to be disposed of.

Regarding forms B and C, we must return to the procedure outlined earlier for registering death. You will have told the doctor who issues the medical certificate of the cause of death that the deceased is to be cremated. He sees the body and completes form B. He then approaches a second doctor who sees the deceased and who then completes form C, confirming the cause of death. The fee payable to each doctor is paid by the funeral director who adds this to his bill.

In certain circumstances, the doctor will not need to get form C completed. He need only fill in form B if the deceased died while a hospital in-patient and an experienced pathologist has conducted a post-mortem examination and given your doctor the results.

In other circumstances, neither form B nor C is necessary. Where the death is reported to a coroner, tell him straight away that the body is to be cremated. When the coroner has dealt with matters, he will then normally issue a certificate for cremation (form E).

Form F is completed by yet another doctor connected with the crematorium. He is usually a local doctor with this as one of his responsibilities. The funeral director will see that this doctor receives either the coroner's certificate or forms B and C. The 'crematorium doctor' has to be satisfied from looking at forms B and C that everything is in order. Should any complication arise at this point, your funeral director will advise you.

When a stillborn child is to be cremated, only two forms are necessary. The doctor who examined the body or was at the still birth fills in a special form stating that the child was stillborn (form 35). The doctor connected with the crematorium completes form F.

Arrangements made by the funeral director

Local Authorities are responsible for the running of most crematoria and appoint a superintendent in charge.

The funeral director will contact the superintendent, giving sufficient notice for him to agree a time for the cremation. This will be on a weekday as crematoria do not usually operate at weekends. The funeral director will pay all the costs of cremation and pass these on in the bill.

The crematorium chapel is non-denominational. But the funeral director will arrange with a clergyman or other officiator to lead a service if required and pay him on your behalf.

When he has gone through the proposed procedures for the funeral with you, the funeral director should be able to give an itemized list of the charges involved.

Should the deceased have worn a heart pacemaker, this has to be removed by the doctor before cremation for safety reasons. The doctor will make a charge for this and pass the cost to the funeral director who will add it to his bill.

The cremation ceremony

Once the time of the cremation and any ceremony has been confirmed, it will be possible to establish what time the funeral will start, and inform mourners accordingly of all details of the funeral.

This normally begins where the body is, at the funeral parlour or at home. The body can be taken to the church and the mourners will meet there later. The coffin may be taken to the church the evening before the cremation and be placed before the altar to await the service the following day. If the deceased is at a funeral parlour which has its own chapel, a service can be held there before the body is taken to the crematorium.

Should the funeral director be arranging cars for the family, relatives and others, he will ensure that the cortège is formed at the appropriate time.

When the body is taken to the crematorium the service

may have already been held elsewhere. In this case only words of commital will be said at the at the crematorium itself.

On the other hand the service may be held at the crematorium chapel. The coffin is placed on a rest called a catafalque and the ceremony ends with the words of commital.

At this point, in some crematoria, the mourners leave the chapel with the coffin left in view. In others the coffin is at this moment obscured by a curtain or is drawn through a hatch.

From the chapel, the coffin goes into a commital room where it awaits cremation in a special individual furnace.

Let the funeral director know if his services are needed after the ceremony. For instance, his cars may be required to take mourners to a restaurant or to your home or that of a relative for refreshments.

The ashes

When the deceased is cremated, the ashes of the body and the coffin are collected from the individual furnace and kept in a container if relatives wish to keep the remains.

The ashes are usually ready to collect a couple of days after the ceremony. Or for a fee they can be posted to the person who applied for the cremation. On the other hand, the funeral director may collect the ashes and post them to you or keep them for you until their disposal.

The crematorium issues a certificate with the ashes, which will be needed if the ashes are to be scattered or buried. The certificate goes to the church or cemetery authorities concerned.

In some crematoria there is a walled cloister with niches where ashes can be placed. Others have a garden where ashes can be buried or scattered.

The funeral director will be able to go through the various possibilities with you, the degree or lack of ceremony desired and the possibilities of memorials such as a plaque in a crematorium garden. He should also be able to give an estimate of the costs involved.

Information about the beliefs and funeral rituals of Buddhists, Hindus, Muslims, Jews, Sikhs and those with secular views can be obtained from the following organizations:

The Buddhist Society
Hriram Temple (Hindu)
The Islamic Cultural Centre
The Jewish Joint Burial Society
United Synagogue (Orthodox Jews)
The Sikh Temple
The National Secular Society
The British Humanist Association

7   Financial Matters

Paying for the funeral

There are several ways in which funeral expenses can be met. The costs may be covered by the deceased. If the deceased had a joint account with say a spouse, the surviving spouse can continue to use the joint account and may meet funeral expenses from it. However, if the dead person had an individual account it will be frozen.

Up to £5,000 may be paid from the deceased's National Savings to the deceased's executors without a grant being taken out. Get form DNS 904 from the Post Office and return it with a certificate for 'certain statutory purposes'. Similarly up to £5,000 may be obtained from the deceased's pension fund or friendly society by writing to them for the necessary form and returning it with the certificate for 'certain statutory purposes'. However, in all of these cases the payment from the deceased's savings is discretionary and a grant may be required.

The deceased might have been living in a residential home or in a hospital. The possessions in such cases will be handed over to the nearest relative. Also, if the person dealing with the will gives written authority to another person to collect the property it can be handed over. There is an upper limit set by the local authority concerned to the amount which can be handed over in this way.

Among the dead person's papers may be papers or letters from previous employers concerning an occupational pension scheme.

Some such schemes pay a lump sum to help towards funeral costs (and may also provide a pension for any surviving spouse or others).

The deceased person's trade union, professional body or other association or a provident club may pay out a lump sum (and/or pension) at death.

A life insurance policy on the death of the deceased before a certain age may provide a certain amount which may be used towards funeral costs.

If the deceased was a member of a cremation society, you might get reduced cremation fees or some payment towards the costs of cremation.

It may be that money is not available from any of the above sources. Additionally, you may be on a low income so that there is not enough money to pay for the funeral.

Assuming that you are responsible for arranging the funeral, and you or your partner are receiving income support or family credit or housing benefit, you may be able to get help from the social fund. It is part of the social security system and will pay for the cost of a simple funeral within the United Kingdom.

The funeral includes the following:

1 Bringing the body home if the deceased died away from home (but within the United Kingdom).
2 One return journey either to arrange the funeral or to attend it.
3 The death certificate.
4 An ordinary coffin.
5 A car for the coffin and bearers and one following car.
6 Flowers from the person arranging the funeral.
7 Fees for a simple funeral for the funeral director, chaplain and organist.
8 Cemetery or crematorium fees (for a simple funeral).
9 A contribution towards extra costs incurred because of the religion of the deceased. (The DSS will tell you the current amount awarded for this.)

In order to claim money from the social fund, you have to apply within three months of the date of the funeral to your local social security or health and social security office. The staff can send an application form (form SF200) or if preferred they can arrange an interview with you.

As a result you may get a payment. But the money has to be paid back from any of the deceased's estate. This does not include personal possessions or a house which the deceased left to a spouse.

You may be arranging the funeral, but not dealing with the deceased's estate. If so, when the payment for the funeral is made to you from the social fund, the office will write to the person who is responsible for the estate.

Help of a similar kind is available when a war pensioner dies in certain circumstances. You can claim a grant for the cost of a simple funeral if one of the following circumstances is applicable:

1 The war pensioner died from the disablement for which he or she was receiving the pension.
2 The war pensioner died in hospital while receiving treatment for the pensioned disablement.
3 The war pensioner was entitled to constant attendance allowance.

The grant is given absolutely and does not have to be paid back. The claim has to be made within three months of the date of the funeral.

Another source of help if relatives cannot pay for a funeral is the local council.

If the deceased died in a local authority home for the elderly or disabled, or in temporary accommodation, the local council may arrange the funeral. In fact they are duty bound to arrange burial or cremation if no other arrangements are possible.

Finally, the health authority may arrange a funeral of someone who died in hospital. They would need to establish that relatives could not afford to pay and they may claim back the expense from the deceased's estate, if there is one.

Social security benefits

You may be entitled to claim social security benefits when

someone dies. Details of these are set out in various leaflets which will be mentioned in this section.

The leaflet FB29 'Help When Someone Dies' is particularly useful. Leaflet D49 'What to do after a Death' also contains much helpful information.

Widows

There are several sources of help for widows:

1 Widow's payment
2 Widowed mother's allowance
3 Maternity benefits
4 Widow's pension
5 Retirement pension
6 Invalidity benefit
7 Industrial death benefit

Entitlement to these payments may depend on various factors such as your age, the national insurance (NI) contributions paid by your husband, and the number of children living with you.

A shortfall in your husband's NI contributions may mean that you cannot claim a full pension. However, if he died after 11 April 1988 owing to a work accident or industrial disease, the Department of Social Security will take it that he had a full contribution record.

We can now look at each of the sources of help for widows listed above:

1 Widow's payment

This may be due to you if your husband died on 11 April 1988 or after. It is a tax-free lump sum paid immediately your husband dies, so long as your husband paid sufficient NI contributions and you were under 60 years old or your husband was under 65, at the time of death.

You should complete form BW1 obtainable from the social security office. For further information about widow's payment, consult leaflet NP45 'A Guide to

Widows' Benefits'. You may have been receiving a retirement pension when your husband died. If so, read leaflet F85 'Retiring? Your Pension and Other Benefits'.

2 Widowed mother's allowance

You may have one or more children for whom you can get child benefit. Or you may be expecting a baby by your late husband. If so, you could be entitled to widowed mother's allowance, which should be paid automatically by the social security office. There is an allowance for you and extra for each child for whom you previously received child benefit.

You may also be entitled to an extra pension. Leaflet NP45 'A Guide to Widows' Benefits' gives further information on this allowance.

3 Maternity Benefits

If you are pregnant there are three benefits which need to be considered.

Statutory Maternity Pay (SMP) is paid by your employer. You must have been in the same employment for six months or more without a break up to the twenty-sixth week of pregnancy. Also, your average weekly earnings must exceed the threshold where you have to begin paying NI contributions. If both of these conditions are met, you can apply.

Maternity allowance may be payable if you cannot get SMP. To work out whether you are eligible for this payment, first note the week in which your baby is due and count fifteen weeks back from that. You then need to consider the year preceding that date. If in that year you paid full rate NI contributions for six months or more, you should apply.

Maternity payment may be paid from the social fund if you are receiving income support or family credit. Leaflet FB8 'Babies and Benefits' gives further information.

4 Widow's pension

This should be paid to you automatically, if you are

entitled to it, by the social security office.

To be eligible for the pension you have to have been 45 or over with no dependent children when your husband died. Also, you may get it if you are 45 or over when widowed mother's allowance finishes. Should you retire at 60, then retirement pension takes the place of Widow's Pension.

The amount of pension is worked out according to your age when your husband died or when widowed mother's allowance finishes. Leaflet NP45 'A Guide to Widows' Benefits' gives further details.

5 Retirement pension

When your husband died, both of you may have been receiving retirement pension. If so, you may be able to use his NI contributions to gain extra pension.

The registrar will give you form BD8 when you register the death. This should be completed and sent to the social security office. Leaflet FB6 'Retiring? Your Pension and Other Benefits' explains further.

6 Invalidity benefit

There are two sets of circumstances in which you may qualify for invalidity benefit.

First of all, you may have been incapable of working for twenty-eight weeks when your widow's allowance (or widowed mother's allowance) finished. You may not be entitled to a widow's pension or be entitled to less than the full rate because of your age. In this set of circumstances, you can apply for invalidity benefit based on your husband's NI contributions.

Secondly, you may be under 45 and not entitled to widowed mother's allowance. Also you may have been incapable of work at the time your husband died. Again, you may be entitled to invalidity benefit.

When you retire or reach 65, this benefit is replaced by retirement pension.

In order to claim, if you are an employee, ask your employer for form SSP1T or SSP1E. If you are unemployed, form SC1 should be used. As well as being obtainable from the social security office, this form is available from hospitals and doctors. When you claim, a doctor's statement should be enclosed. Leaflet NI 16A 'Invalidity Benefit' gives further information.

7 Industrial death benefit

Your husband may have died as a result of an accident at work or from an industrial disease. If death occurred before 11 April 1988, you may be entitled to industrial death benefit and form BW1 should be used to claim.

Your husband may have died as a result of one of several diseases including pneumoconiosis or byssinosis. He may have contracted the disease at work before 5 July 1948. If so, complete the form on the back of leaflet PN1, 'Pneumoconiosis, byssinosis and some other diseases from work before 5 July 1948'. The social security office have copies.

Relatives of war pensioners

There are two forms of help which are available to relatives of war pensioners: war pensions for widows and War pensions for other relatives.

1 War pensions for widows

This pension is paid in any one of three circumstances:

(i) Your husband's death was a result of service in the armed forces within certain dates. These dates are between 1914 and 1921 and after 2 September 1939.
(ii) Your husband's death resulted from a war injury in the 1939–45 war. He was a merchant seaman or a civilian at the time of the injury.
(iii) At the time of his death, your husband was

entitled to a constant attendance allowance under the war pension scheme.

The amount you get depends on three factors, your age, your husband's armed forces rank, and the number of children you have.

Your husband may have been receiving constant attendance allowance or unemployability supplement. If so, you will receive a special temporary allowance for the first twenty-six weeks after his death. You get this no matter what the cause of death.

You may be entitled to the NI Widow's Payment. In this event, your temporary allowance is reduced by the amount of the widow's payment. The reduction is spread across the twenty-six weeks. However, the temporary allowance will not be allowed to fall below the level of war widow's pension plus widow's payment.

Leaflet MPL 152 'War Widows' gives further information. Leaflet MPL 154 'Rates of War Pensions and Allowances' gives current rates.

2 War pensions for other relatives

War pensions to certain other relatives may be paid. The deceased must have died as a result of:

    (i)   service in the Armed forces or
    (ii)   injury as a civilian or merchant seaman in the 1939–45 war

The relatives who may be paid war pension are the deceased's children, parents, widower or other near relatives. Leaflet MPL 152 'War Widows' gives more information. Leaflet MPL 154 'Rates of War Pensions and Allowances' gives current rates.

Widowers

Three kinds of help available to widowers are as follows:

1 Retirement Pension
2 Invalidity Benefit
3 Industrial Death Benefit

If you are a widower, you may be entitled to benefits relating to your wife's NI contributions.

1 Retirement pension

You may be a widower getting a retirement pension at lower than the full rate. If so, you may be able to increase the amount by using your deceased wife's contributions.

Should your wife have been over 60 when she died, you might get a larger pension.

On the other hand you may be unable to get a retirement pension at the moment. Your wife's contributions may assist you in getting one.

Claim on form BD8 and send it to the social security office.

Leaflet FB6 'Retiring? Your Pension and Other Benefits' gives further information.

2 Invalidity benefit

You may have been incapable of work when your wife died. Or you may have become incapable of work within thirteen weeks of your wife's death and remained so for at least twenty-eight weeks. In either of these circumstances, you could be entitled to invalidity benefit based on your wife's NI contributions.

When you reach 70, retirement pension replaces invalidity benefit.

If you are an employee, your employer can give you form SSP 1T or form SSP 1E on which to claim. Otherwise , you should use form SC1.

A doctor's statement should be enclosed in support of your claim.

Leaflets NI 16A 'Invalidity Benefit' and NI 16 'Sickness Benefit' give further information.

3 Industrial death benefit

Your wife may have died as a result of a work accident or an industrial disease.

If the following conditions are met, you may be entitled to Industrial Death Benefit:

    (i)   Death occurred before 11 April 1988
   (ii)   Your wife financially supported you
  (iii)   You are not able to support yourself.

Claim on form BI200 available from the Social Security Office.

It may be that your wife died as a result of pneumoconiosis or byssinosis or one of certain other diseases. The disease may have been contracted as a consequence of work done before 5 July 1948. If all these are the case you should claim on Form PN1A. This is part of leaflet PN1 available from the social security office.

One parent families

While you may not be entitled to widow's benefit, you may be rearing a child alone. If so, you may be able to get one parent benefit.

Get the leaflet CH11 'One Parent Benefit' from your social security office. Attached to it is a claim form.

Other benefits which can be claimed are income support, family credit or housing benefit. These are explained later in this chapter.

Guardian's allowance

Guardian's allowance can be claimed if you take an orphan into your home and family and receive child benefit for him or her. The term orphan is usually taken to indicate that both the child's parents are dead. Sometimes the allowance is paid when only one parent is dead.

You may claim if you are the child's step-parent. You do not need to be the legal guardian. However, you may not claim if you have legally adopted the child.

If you have already applied for child benefit, claim for guardian's allowance as soon as possible afterwards. Should you not yet have applied for child benefit, send in a claim for both. The claim form for guardian's allowance is Form BG1. Leaflet NI 14 'Guardian's Allowance' provides further information.

Insufficient income

Three main sources of help may be available if your income is insufficient to live on. These are income support, family credit, housing benefit

1 Income support

Even if you are working part time or claiming other benefits you can still claim income support. You must meet the following criteria:

(i) Over the age of 16
(ii) Not have over a specified sum in savings (in 1990 this was £6,000)
(iii) Not be working for twenty-four hours or more a week. (Exceptions may be made to this.)

Complete the claim form in leaflet SB1 'Income Support – Cash Help'. Leaflet SB20 'A Guide to Income Support' gives further information.

2 Family credit

If you work for twenty-four hours a week or more and are bringing up a family, you may be able to get family credit.

The local post office or social security office will supply you with the relevant claim form and a prepaid envelope. The form is part of leaflet FC1 'Family Credit' and the benefit is claimed by post.

3 Housing benefit

Your local council may help you with rent or community charge. Help may be available even if you own your own home, have savings and are employed. Claim forms are available at the council office.

The social security office may be able to help with certain other housing expenses. These include help with some of the mortgage interest, some maintenance costs and some insurance expenses.

Leaflet RR1 'Housing Benefit – Help with Rent and Rates' gives more information.

National Health Service costs

If you are receiving income support or family credit, you qualify automatically for certain NHS services or items free:

- Prescriptions
- Dental treatment
- Sight tests and vouchers for spectacles
- Hospital travel costs
- Wigs and fabric supports

Also, if you are on a low income, you may get help towards the services and items listen above. Leaflet AB11 'Help with NHS costs' gives more information.

Tax

Social security benefits may not be free of tax. An extra tax allowance exists for widows. Leaflet IR23 'Income Tax and Widows' gives more information. As well as being obtainable from the social security office, this leaflet is available from the registrar or the tax office.

There is also an extra tax allowance if you are raising a child alone. Leaflet IR29 'Income Tax and One-Parent Families' gives further details.

Expected and peaceful death

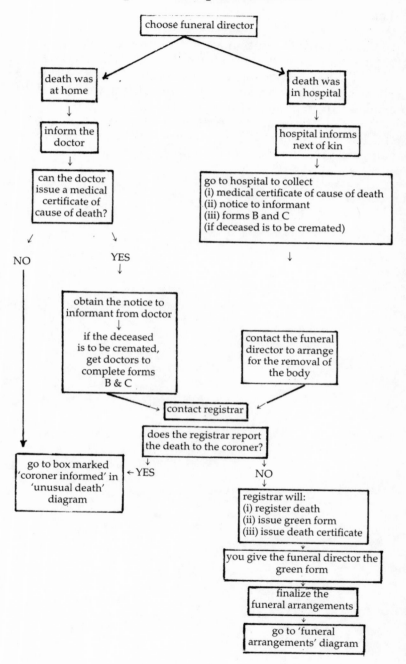

Unusual death

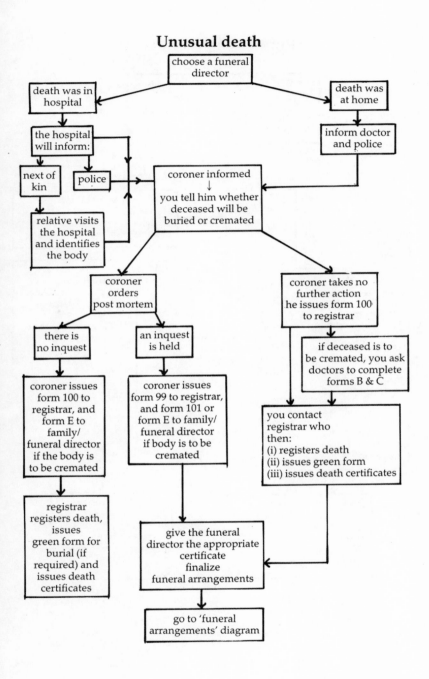

Funeral arrangements

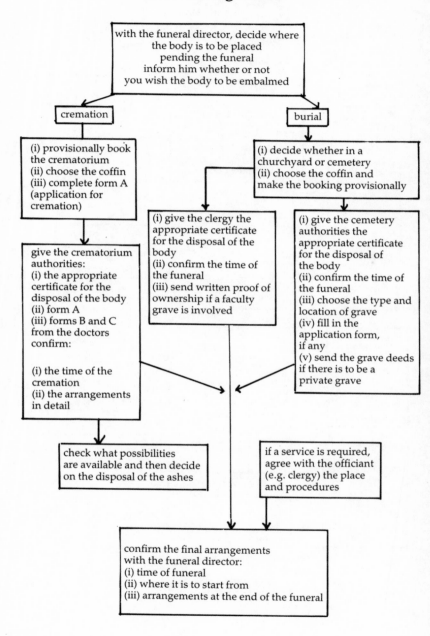

with the funeral director, decide where
the body is to be placed
pending the funeral
inform him whether or not
you wish the body to be embalmed

cremation

burial

(i) provisionally book
the crematorium
(ii) choose the coffin
(iii) complete form A
(application for
cremation)

(i) decide whether in a
churchyard or cemetery
(ii) choose the coffin and
make the booking provisionally

(i) give the clergy the
appropriate certificate
for the disposal of the
body
(ii) confirm the time of
the funeral
(iii) send written proof of
ownership if a faculty
grave is involved

(i) give the cemetery
authorities the
appropriate certificate
for the disposal of
the body
(ii) confirm the time of
the funeral
(iii) choose the type and
location of grave
(iv) fill in the
application form,
if any
(v) send the grave deeds
if there is to be a
private grave

give the crematorium
authorities:
(i) the appropriate
certificate for the
disposal of the body
(ii) form A
(iii) forms B and C
from the doctors
confirm:

(i) the time of the
cremation
(ii) the arrangements
in detail

check what possibilities
are available and then decide
on the disposal of the ashes

if a service is required,
agree with the officiant
(e.g. clergy) the place
and procedures

confirm the final arrangements
with the funeral director:
(i) time of funeral
(ii) where it is to start from
(iii) arrangements at the end of the funeral

Part 2

The Deceased's Estate

8 When There is No Will

Intestacy

A will is no more than a record of the deceased person's wishes about certain things he would like done after his death.

Whilst it is always advisable for a person to make a will, not everyone does so. Sometimes this is because it is hard to face up to our own mortality, or it could be that death comes unexpectedly early. Whatever the reason, relatives may be faced with the prospect of trying to sort out the deceased's affairs when no will has been made.

When there is no will, the deceased is said to have died 'intestate'. Someone, perhaps the deceased's nearest relative, acts as a 'personal representative'. He deals with the deceased's estate, that is, all the property which the deceased has left.

The nearest relatives may apply for a 'grant of letters of administration'. Should the closest relative not want to apply, he can decline. The responsibility is then passed down along the line of relatives.

First in line is the surviving spouse. If there is no widow or widower or if they decline to apply, the responsibility is passed down the line in the following order: children, grandchildren, parents, brothers and sisters or their children, and half-brothers and half-sisters or their children.

After these come grandparents, uncles and aunts or their children and finally uncles and aunts of half blood or their children.

It makes no difference in the rules of intestacy whether

the relationships are 'natural', adoptive or illegitimate.

A child who is adopted has the same rights of inheritance as the natural children of his adoptive parents. However, an adopted child loses any rights of inheritance from his own natural parents, and those natural parents lose their rights under intestacy laws.

The estate has to be disposed of according to certain rules. The first claim on the estate is by those to whom the deceased owed something. Funeral debts are included in this category.

Any remaining estate is divided amongst family members following the provisions of the Administration of Estates Act 1925.

Inheritance Tax is paid according to how intestacy rules distribute the property.

For instance, no tax is payable on property which goes to a surviving spouse because the spouse exemption rule applies. Bands of exclusion apply to other beneficiaries as will be explained later.

Sharing the estate

Let us consider some of the various situations that can arise when the deceased dies intestate.

The estate of an unmarried person (or where there is no surviving spouse) with children is shared equally among the children. If any child has died, their share goes to their children. The estate of an unmarried person without children goes to the parents. If both parents are dead, the deceased's estate is shared by his brothers and sisters. Where there are no sisters or brothers the deceased's grandparents benefit. If they are dead the aunts and uncles of the deceased share the estate. Next come nephews and nieces and then cousins. It is worth noting that the first claim after parents is the children of those parents, that is the deceased's brothers and sisters. Similarly, the children of those in the chain of potential claimants: brothers and sisters, grandparents, aunts and uncles may also have a claim on the estate. This arises if their own parent has died but would have had a claim on the estate had they survived the deceased. For instance, assume the deceased had one brother and no sisters and the brother died before the deceased, leaving offspring. That offspring would be entitled to the share of the estate that would have gone to his father, had his father lived.

If neither grandparents nor any of their descendants survive the deceased's estate becomes the property of the Crown 'in bona vacantia'.

The procedure described above applies whether the deceased is an unmarried man or an unmarried woman.

If the deceased is divorced, the estate is shared as if there were no surviving spouse.

If a couple are married, the procedure is different when one of them dies.

Consider the case where the total possessions of the partner who dies amounts to a figure under a certain threshold.

> *In 1990 the threshold was*
> *£75,000.*

Whether or not there are children, the whole amount goes to the surviving partner, plus any interest and personal possessions.

What happens if the total value of the estate exceeds the threshold? It depends whether or not there are children. If there are, then the surviving spouse is allowed the threshold amount and the household effects and personal effects of the deceased. Should the house itself be valued at more than the threshold amount, the surviving spouse is not automatically entitled to keep the house.

What remains of the estate is shared in two ways. Half is shared equally among the children, being held for them if they are under 18 years old, until they reach that age. Half goes into 'trust'. This means that the surviving spouse may not draw on the capital value of this part of the estate, but can receive income from it. When the surviving spouse dies, the capital reverts to the children.

If there are no children, the surviving partner is entitled

to a larger amount if the estate is big enough.

In 1990, this was £125,000.

In addition, the surviving spouse receives the following:

● household effects
● the deceased's personal effects
● plus half of the remainder of the estate

The other half of the remainder of the estate goes to the deceased's parents, brothers and sisters or their children, if they are still alive. If not, the whole estate goes to the surviving spouse. These rules apply whether the deceased is the wife or the husband.

The range of rules described above apply to anyone who at the time of death was domiciled in England or Wales. A country of domicile is the one which a person regards as his permanent home.

It may not necessarily be the country in which he dies. Someone dying abroad while on holiday would still be considered domiciled in say England if that was normally his permanent home.

The rules regarding intestacy if the deceased dies domiciled in Scotland are described in a later chapter.

Obtaining current figures

Under intestacy, relevant figures can vary from time to time and should be checked. Current figures are obtained from the citizens advice bureau or local library.

Circumstances	Amount given in our examples	Enter current figures
The threshold under which, in the case of a married couple where one dies intestate, the whole amount goes to the surviving partner irrespective of whether there are children	£75,000	
For a married couple, if one dies intestate and there are no children, the surviving spouse's entitlement to the estate (where certain other relatives of the deceased were still alive)	£125,000 + household effects + personal effects + ½ the remaining estate	

9   Inheritance Tax

Lifetime gifts

On the death of a person whose domicile is in the United Kingdom a liability to inheritance tax (IHT) can arise. Generally the tax affects property passing from a deceased person to beneficiaries under his will or intestacy on the deceased's death.

But even certain gifts which someone gives in his lifetime incur IHT. Among these are a gift to a discretionary trust, in which trustees hold property and decide who benefits. A gift to a company also falls within the IHT remit. Both of these incur tax at half of the rate which would be payable at death.

Lifetime gifts are by no means always subject to IHT and the following do not normally attract it:

1 A gift made from one person to another
2 A gift to a trust through which someone else is entitled to income
3 A gift to a disabled person
4 A gift to a trust which benefits children regarding their education and maintenance.

However, such gifts may involve liability for income tax and capital gains tax, and legal advice should be taken about this.

Also, such gifts may be subject to IHT under the so called seven year rule. This is meant to prevent someone avoiding paying IHT by giving all his property away before he dies.

Tax is payable according to the time which has elapsed

between the transfer of property and death. Tax bands mean that, the closer the death is to the seven year exemption point, the lower the tax level will be.

The effect of this is that, if you have received a gift from the deceased in the seven years before he died, then, on the deceased's death, tax on the gift becomes due.

> *The following table shows the relevant rates in 1990/91.*

As these rates may be changed from year to year, it is essential to get the most up-to-date table for calculations of IHT due. The capital taxes office will provide these. These rates are the ones current when the deceased died, irrespective of what the rates were for the year in which the gifts were given.

Rates of IHT, current at 1990/91, due on the deceased's death after a taxable lifetime gift has been received

within 3 years	100%
between 3 and 4 years	80%
between 4 and 5 years	60%
between 5 and 6 years	40%
between 6 and 7 years	20%
more than 7 years	0%

Some lifetime gifts are exempt from tax. Small gifts given to a particular person in any one year are exempt.

> *In 1990, a small gift was defined as one up to the value of £250.*

Wedding gifts may be exempt, even if they exceed the value set for small gifts. It depends on the closeness of the relationship between donor and recipient.

Larger gifts up to a certain value which are given to one person or several are exempt from all tax in any one year.

> *The maximum value allowed in 1990 was £3,000.*

If in one year, a gift of less than the allowed amount is given, then the following year, once the amount allowed for that current year is used up, the shortfall from the previous year can be carried forward.

> *Take an example using the 1990 figure of an allowed £3,000. Assume a gift of £2,000 is given in one year. The year following, the £3,000 allowed for that year can be given and once that is used up, the £1,000 shortfall from the previous year may be given. The allowance cannot be carried forward for more than one year.*

When property is given as a lifetime gift, its value will be assessed on the death of the benefactor, according to what it was worth when it was originally given. It may have increased in value or have yielded an income. Therefore, even if the donor dies within three years of giving the gift there could still be a saving on IHT overall.

Lifetime gifts which attract tax under the seven year rule and tax-exempt gifts can both have a bearing on the IHT which is paid on the deceased's estate at death.

The value of all the chargeable lifetime gifts given by the deceased in the seven years before he died is totalled. Any gifts which are exempt are deducted from this. The remaining value is included as part of the deceased's estate for the purpose of calculating IHT payable at death.

Inheritance tax at death

Inheritance tax rate

IHT, as we have seen, is essentially concerned with property going from one person to another.

It is charged on the value of the net estate of the

deceased. This net estate is what is left of the estate once debts and liabilities have been honoured. Included in the estate's value is the capital value of all of the deceased's property which falls into the three categories which follow:

1 Property in which the deceased had a life interest
2 Property from which he benefited
3 Property entitling him to income

Up to a specified limit an estate attracts no IHT.

> *In 1990 the first £128,000 of an estate attracted no IHT.*

Above that amount, 40% tax is charged. Both the amount allowed before any tax is deducted and the rate of tax may be changed each year. So up-to-date figures must be obtained at the time of death.

Exemptions from IHT

Not everything is included in the total when IHT is calculated, however, for there are certain exemptions from tax. Some of these are as follows:

1 Property given by one spouse to another
2 Gifts willed to charity
3 Gifts willed to main political parties
4 An unlimited number of separate small gifts

> *In 1990 up to £250 per recipient was allowed.*

5 Larger gifts of up to a certain value in each year

> *In 1990 the upper limit was £3,000 per year.*

6 Special cases where legal advice should be sought, and

where part exemption from IHT may be gained. These include property such as farmland, forestry and partnership businesses.

Deeds of variation

Through an arrangement known as a deeds of variation or deeds of family arrangement, beneficiaries of the deceased's estate may vary the provisions of the will. This must be done within two years of the deceased's death. The idea is that the deceased's property passes to beneficiaries in a more tax-effective way.

For example, assume a husband and wife have willed their property to each other when one dies. They have an adult son. The husband dies leaving his property to his wife. But she also dies within two years leaving everything to her son. The son may save IHT by obtaining a deed of variation for his father's will.

Take for instance the threshold applicable in 1990, which was £128,000. Assume the father's estate was £130,000 and the mother's estate was another £130,000.

If a deed of variation was not considered, the father's estate would pass to the mother at his death attracting no IHT because it is a transfer of property between husband and wife. The total estate of £260,000 would pass to the son on his mother's death. The first £128,000 would attract no IHT but the remaining £132,000 could be liable to 40% IHT.

But what happens if, on the death of his mother, the son arranges a deed of variation on his father's will so that his father's estate passes directly to him? The first £128,000 of the father's estate would be free of IHT and 40% would be payable on the remaining. The same would apply to his mother's estate, where IHT would be payable only on £2,000. By arranging deeds of variation, IHT is due on £4,000 rather than £132,000, a considerable saving.

If you think such an arrangement might be appropriate, seek legal advice.

Jointly owned property

What is the position if the deceased jointly owned property, say a house?

The beneficiary to the deceased's share of the property may incur tax.

A spouse would avoid IHT under rules exempting IHT on property passing between husband and wife. However, a son, daughter, parent or friend would be liable for tax on that share of the property which passed from the deceased. The beneficiary may be the co-owner of the house or he may not.

Lifetime gifts and IHT at death

When assessing IHT due on an estate, the value of all chargeable lifetime gifts also have a bearing.

Remember that up to a certain threshold, no IHT is due at the deceased's death.

In 1990 this threshold was £128,000.

Part or all of this threshold may be used up by lifetime gifts under the seven year rule.

In this example we will use the 1990 IHT exemption threshold of £128,000 for an estate left on the deceased's death.

Assume a father (a widower) gives a lifetime gift of £153,000 to his son. The father dies within 3 years leaving a further £100,000 to his son in his will.

Under the list of exemptions from IHT given earlier, larger gifts up to a certain value are exempt. Let us take the 1990 figure of a £3,000 exemption threshold.

> *This means that £3,000 of the £153,000 lifetime gift*
> *does not attract IHT.*
> *Next, consider the rates of IHT due at the deceased's*
> *death after a taxable lifetime gift has been received. IHT*
> *becomes due on 100% of the lifetime gift if the deceased*
> *dies within 3 years of giving it.*
> *So £150,000 of the lifetime gift becomes the focus of*
> *IHT. A certain amount is exempt. In 1990 figures,*
> *£128,000 would be free of IHT, and the remaining*
> *£22,000 would attract 40% IHT.*
> *Taxable lifetime gifts are included in the deceased's*
> *estate. So the £100,000 left in the will is all taxed at the*
> *40% rate, the £128,000 exemption being already used*
> *up.*

Legacy and residue

A will may specify that a legacy is left to someone and the
residue left to someone else. The residue is what remains
of an estate when debts and taxes have been paid and
legacies made.

A legacy may be given subject to taxes due or free from
taxes. If the legacy is mentioned in the will using the
following words: 'subject to the payment of all taxes and
duties by reference to my death' this means that the
amount which the legacy specified, say £200,000, will be
subject to the appropriate amount of IHT. The amount of
the legacy is then clearly predictable.

The situation is different if the will specifies that the
legacy is 'free from all taxes and duties payable on or by
reference to my death'. Also, if the will does not specify
either, then it is assumed that any legacy is to be free of
taxes and duties. In such cases, the amount to be paid as a
legacy, say £200,000 again, has to have had tax already on
it paid.

For tax purposes, tax due on a legacy constitutes part of
that legacy. So an amount has to be calculated gross,
which will leave a net of £200,000, after tax has been paid,
for the legacy. In a sense, tax comes out of the residue thus

reducing the amount of the residue.

You can get tables from the Inland Revenue which enable the gross and net calculations to be made.

Obtaining current figures

The following rates and figures may change from time to time so current figures should be obtained from the citizens advice bureau or capital taxes offices

	Rates from our examples	Enter Current Rates
1 Rates of IHT due at the deceased's death after a taxable lifetime gift has been received	see rates of IHT given earlier	
2 The limit of a small lifetime gift exempt from IHT	£250	
3 The limit for a larger lifetime gift exempt from IHT in any one year	£3,000	
4 The limit of an estate's value under which IHT is exempt	£128,000	
5 The rate of IHT above the exemption threshold	40%	
6 The value limit of 'small' gifts left to different people in a will	£250	
7 The value limit of larger gifts left in a will for any one year	£3,000	

10 The Will and Probate

Introduction

A will, as we have already noted, is a record of the wishes of a person about certain things he would like done after his death.

Before looking at the will in more detail, it will now be useful to define rather more precisely what a will is.

For a will to be valid a person has to incorporate in a legally valid document his intentions concerning the disposition of his property on his death.

A will does not take effect until the testator dies. Also it is effective to dispose of the property which the testator owns at the date the will is made and also all the property which he acquires between the date of the will and his death. A will must be revokable at any time before the testator dies. It can effectively dispose of all the testator's property of whatever kind.

Here we are concerned with how you deal with the will of someone for whom you may be executor. The will may have been kept in the deceased's home in a locked drawer, in a safe or in some other secure repository.

The document may have been placed at a bank. Should this be the case, the executor may collect it personally and sign for it. Or he can ask for it to be posted to him and send the bank a written acknowledgement that it has been received.

There may be more than one executor. If so the bank may release the will to one executor but would require that in due course all of the executors would make a written acknowledgement.

The layout of the will

A will normally has three parts.

The first covers the appointment of a person (or more than one person) to handle the deceased's affairs. This person, the executor, might be a relative of the deceased, a friend, or a solicitor. Also included in this part are such matters as the deceased's wishes for his funeral and arrangements for any children to be looked after by guardians.

The second part of the will is the main part. It concerns the distribution of the deceased's property or estate. This might include, for example, leaving a house to someone, specified amounts of money to another and particular possessions to yet another.

The final part deals with administrative matters to help the executor fulfil his obligations concerning the will.

Naturally, the exact form and content of a will varies from person to person. But there are several common features which often occur.

(i) The heading

A common heading would be as follows:

'This is the last will and testament of me John Green of 10 Ash Road, Boxhill, Herefordshire made this eleventh day of January one thousand nine hundred and ninety one.'

Or the heading may be rather simpler:

'The will of John Green of 10 Ash Road, Boxhill, Herefordshire.'

(ii) Revocation clause

The following clause is used, even if no previous wills (and codicils) have been made.

'I hereby revoke all former wills and codicils made by me and declare this to be my last will.'

It saves relatives looking unnecessarily for any previous wills, because, even if any had been made and were found, the most recent will revokes them.

A codicil is an amendment to a will which alters part of it but not all, saving the effort of redrafting the whole will. By revoking all previous codicils, the most recent will again avoids confusion and unnecessary speculation about possible prior codicils.

(iii) Naming the executor(s)

The will may appoint one or more executors. It may make provision for the possibility that, if the executor is a wife or husband or grown up child of the deceased, they may be killed in a common accident. It may specify alternative executors should the initial choice be unable or unwilling to act. The will might read as follows:

(a) 'I appoint as my executors my wife Margaret if she survives me by thirty days and my friend David Albert Brown of 20 Ash Road, Boxhill, Herefordshire.

(b) 'If my wife Margaret dies before me or does not survive me for thirty days then my friend David Albert Brown of 20 Ash Road, Boxhill, Herefordshire is to be my sole executor.'

The choice of the period of thirty days is somewhat arbitrary. Say there is a common accident to John and Margaret Green, and John is killed. Then it is hoped that, if Margaret survives for thirty days she would make a full recovery and be able to assume the role of joint executor.

(iv) Appointing guardians for children

Both husband and wife may die within a short space of time as a result of a common accident or for some other reason. With this eventuality in mind, the deceased may have specified, in the will, arrangements for the care of his children.

Where this is done, it is usual for the guardians to be named as executors or joint executors with another person.

The relevant clause in the will of Michael Chappel a married man with a wife and infant children, might read as follows:

'If my wife Audrey dies before me or does not survive me for thirty days then I appoint Donald and Joan Fairchild to be the guardians of my infant children Ruth and Andrew.'

Where such arrangements have been made, the will may make a provision for part of the estate to be placed in trust for the benefit of the surviving children.

(v) Instructions about disposing of the body

Instructions about the disposal of the body will usually specify either burial or cremation.

If the deceased wishes certain organs or his body to be donated to medical science, this will be indicated. Two examples might be:

'I wish my kidneys to be donated for medical purposes and my body to be buried.'
'I wish my body to be donated for medical purposes and my body to be afterwards cremated.'

This clause of the will is not essential.

(vi) Bequests

A bequest is a legacy of some property other than houses or land. It might be an antique, a musical instrument, a painting or some other item.

Before the bequests are itemized in the will, there may be a clause specifying that the items are given free of taxes and duties incurred.

'I give the following bequests free from all taxes and duties payable on or by reference to my death.'

On the other hand, the will may specify that the bequests are not free from such taxes and duties. In this case, the beneficiary would be liable to pay the appropriate proportion of tax due on the deceased's estate.

The items to be bequeathed are then listed and the beneficiary identified. For example:

1 My gold wedding ring to my daughter Anne
2 My Lowry painting to my friend John Barket of 257 Fitzwilliam Drive, Doncaster

(vii) Legacies

A legacy is property left to another person by a will. The property may be a house, land, money or any other asset.

As in the case of bequests, the deceased may have specified whether or not the legacy is 'free from all taxes and duties payable on or by reference to my death'. The legacies are then listed and the beneficiaries identified.

If a house with an outstanding mortgage is left to a beneficiary, the will may indicate that it is free of any liability for any outstanding mortgage. This would mean that the mortgage would be paid off as a debt of the deceased's estate.

Should money be left to a charity, a phrase may be added after the name of the charity and the amount to be given, to this effect:

'The receipt of the treasurer or other person professing to be the duly authorized officer shall be a full and sufficient discharge to my executors.'

This is intended to clarify the executor's task and protect you from any disputes about the disposal of the estate.

(iix) The residue

The residue is what is left of the deceased's estate after obligations have been met. These obligations are bequests, legacies, and all taxes and debts. This part of the will might read as follows:

'I leave to my husband Keith the whole of the rest of my estate.'

(ix) Leaving property in trust

A trust may be set up for the benefit of someone, often young children, to be administered by others until the time comes for the beneficiaries to receive their due.

Provision for this may be made in the event of a husband and wife dying in say a common accident and leaving young children. The financial provision could be made by leaving property to specified executors, for instance the guardians named in the will and another person.

(x) Signatures

The date of the will may be written, if it is written at all, at the beginning or end of the document.

At the conclusion of the provisions of the will, may be a phrase such as:

'As witness my hand this tenth day of January one thousand nine hundred and ninety.'

This is followed by the signature of the deceased.

Between this and the signatures of the witnesses may be found another stock phrase, such as:

'Signed by the testator in the presence of us both present at the same time together who in his presence have subscribed our names as witnesses.'

The 'testator' is simply the person making the will. If this is a woman, the term 'testatrix' is used.

The final phrase is followed by the signatures of each of the two witnesses who may also have printed their names for clarity. Beneath each witness's signature is the signatory's address.

Probate

Probate is to do with dealing with a deceased person's property (his estate).

The individual who deals with the estate after the

deceased's death is known as the 'personal representative'. He may be appointed by a will in which case he is called an executor. Normally, he has to get a document from the high court to confirm his legal powers to handle matters. This document is called a grant of probate. The executor does not have to wait for this document in order to act. He has authority to act from the time the deceased dies. This authority is merely confirmed by probate.

On the other hand, the personal representative may not be appointed by a will, which is of course the case if there is no will at all.

He is then called the administrator rather than the executor. He still normally has to get a high court document confirming his lawful authority to deal with the estate. In this case, the document is called a grant of letters of administration. Until this is issued, an administrator lacks the legal power to act.

You may be appointed an executor in the deceased's will. Ideally, the deceased should have talked to you about this and obtained your agreement before entering your name on the will.

If not, or if you feel unable or unwilling for any reason to deal with the responsibilities, you can decline. Alternatively, you can accept and then appoint a solicitor to deal with formalities.

It is worth noting that an executor cannot be made to give up his responsibilities unless he is found to be guilty of misconduct. Where more than one executor is appointed by the will, it is helpful therefore if they work in harmony. Sometimes, one executor may be a member of the deceased's family while the other could be a solicitor or an accountant. If you are a family executor you cannot insist that any other executor, family member or not, leaves the responsibility to you, unless they are guilty of misconduct.

Normally, however, this situation does not arise. Indeed, if there is more than one executor this helps share the work involved. Where there are trusts to set up, for example, the help of another executor, such as a solicitor, would probably be welcomed.

If you have been appointed executor and do not wish to take on all the duties, four broad choices lie open.

First, you can complete a form of renunciation by which you renounce responsibility straight away. These are available from law stationers, such as Oyez.

Secondly, you could instead get a 'power reserved letter' from the probate office which you sign to renounce your role.

In each of these cases, the responsibility is then assumed by the other executor(s) if several were named in the will, or the role may be taken on by a reserve executor specified in the will.

If you sign a power reserved letter, you reserve the right to apply to resume the duties of executor if circumstances dictate. It is possible, for instance, that another executor might die before the estate was sorted out.

The third alternative is to appoint a lawyer to obtain the grant. The lawyer is then empowered to act as if he had been mentioned as an executor in the will. A form which is available from legal stationers enables an executor to do this.

Finally, you can accept the role of executor, obtain the grant, and then employ a lawyer to take over the remaining duties.

You may be nominated as an executor by implication. This happens where the testator does not specifically nominate someone as executor. Instead, the testator requests someone to carry out duties which are usually performed by an executor. The will may say for instance:

'I wish Jean Whitehead to collect my assets and pay my debts.'

A person who is nominated by implication in this way is known as an executor 'according to the tenor'.

No one should meddle with the deceased's property by carrying out duties which are normally performed by a personal representative unless they have

(a) been expressly appointed executor by the will
(b) been impliedly appointed executor by the will ('according to the tenor')
(c) obtained letters of administration

If anyone does so interfere in such a way, he becomes an executor by his own wrong-doing, that is in legal terminology an executor 'de son tort'.

In one sense he is not really an executor and may not apply for a grant of probate. However, because of his wrong-doing he may incur the following penalties:

(a) He may be sued for conversion by the legitimate executor or administrator
(b) He becomes liable for due payment of inheritance tax
(c) He may be sued by the beneficiary of the estate or by creditors

Checking that you are entitled to apply for a grant

To make sure that you are entitled to a grant, check the following carefully:

1 If there is a valid will and you are named as an executor you can apply.
2 If there is a will it may not name executors. Or it may name executors but they are unable or unwilling to apply for a grant. In these circumstances you can apply for a grant if you are named in the will and the deceased gives you all or part of his estate.
3 Should the deceased not have made a valid will, the closest next of kin can apply for a grant. The order of priority is as follows:
   (a) spouse
   (b) sons or daughters, or if any have died in the deceased's lifetime, then grandchildren may apply
   (c) parents
   (d) brothers and sisters, or if any have died in the deceased's lifetime, then nephews and nieces should apply
   (e) more distant relatives

However, a grant cannot be given to anyone under 18 years old. Also, illegitimate relatives (except sons or daughters) may not be entitled to a grant.

A maximum of four applicants are allowed, but normally only one person needs to obtain the grant.

What can be involved in dealing with an estate

The personal representative contacts the deceased's bank and any other institution where the deceased had an account so that cheques, banker's orders and savings accounts can be closed. He also informs the tax inspector of the death.

He takes stock of all the estate's assets and writes to all the necessary institutions. Among the assets may be a house, land, money in a current bank account, bank savings, premium bonds, shares, personal possessions, a car and any unclaimed pension.

He establishes what has to be debited from the estate. Debits might include debts such as any outstanding house mortgage, taxes like inheritance tax, liabilities, funeral costs and the cost of administering the estate.

Assets and liabilities must be itemized to estimate the inheritance tax payable. Because IHT is paid before assets are released, it may be necessary to arrange short term credit to pay the IHT.

The personal representative applies for probate if he is an executor or for letters of administration if he is an administrator. He completes a series of forms in connection with this. He later has to personally visit the probate registry.

He corresponds with the inland revenue to claim any PAYE tax returns and to eventually settle all the deceased's tax affairs.

On receiving probate or letters of administration he sends copies to those who hold the assets, such as the insurance company or bank manager so the assets can be released. He pays off the estate's debts.

He then distributes the remaining property according to the instructions of the will (or the rules of intestacy). Where there is a will, this might mean transferring property such as a house to a beneficiary, paying money to someone specified in the will, or holding property of any kind in trust for someone.

Anything left in the estate following all this is called the residue. The will should specify how this is to be distributed and the personal representative will carry this out.

Particular complications arise where the estate's debts are greater than its assets. A solicitor should be consulted in such cases of insolvency.

Circumstances in which a grant is not required

Sometimes a grant, that is a grant of probate or letter of administration, is *not* required. The following are some of these circumstances:

1 The deceased's property comprises only bank notes and coins and personal possessions such as furniture.
2 The deceased held a certain amount in National Savings. When the date of payment arrives, interest on the savings must not have pushed the balance over the threshold amount. The amount can be paid to the beneficiary.

The specified threshold in 1990 was £5,000.

The same principle applies to money in some pension funds, certain friendly societies and a savings bank.

All the potential beneficiary has to do normally is to write to the organization concerned. He states the circumstances and asks for the relevant form. The form is completed and returned with a death certificate (which is needed for certain statutory purposes). In certain circumstances a photocopy of the marriage certificate will be needed.

In the case of National Savings, the form needed is DNS 904.

3 The property was 'nominated'. This used to be a way of naming certain kinds of property so that it went to a

specified person at the nominator's death. Property such as money in a National Savings Bank account could be nominated. This system ended in 1981 but nominations made before then are valid.

Normally the person nominated has only to show the death certificate in order to have the property transferred to him. But for large amounts, the savings bank may wish to see a certificate from the Inland Revenue showing that IHT has been paid if appropriate.

A nomination can be revoked by:

(a) the nominator signing an appropriate form
(b) the nominee dying before the nominator
(c) the nominator's marriage

The nomination is unaffected by whether or not it is mentioned in a will. It cannot be altered by a will made after the nomination was arranged.

4 The property in the estate is in joint names as joint tenants. When one joint owner dies, the asset passes to the surviving joint owner.

He must provide the authorities concerned with the death certificate. In the case of a joint bank account for example the relevant authority would be the bank.

The surviving joint-owner is liable to pay inheritance tax on half the value of the asset.

Probate may not be required. But if the estate's value exceeds a certain threshold value, the inland revenue require an account of the property of the estate. This must be signed by executors.

The threshold value in 1990 was £100,000.

The value includes all jointly held property, and all taxable gifts given during the ten years prior to death.

When a solicitor should be consulted

A solicitor can be consulted at any point if there are specific issues you are not sure of in administering the estate. His fees would come out of the deceased's estate. Usually the person who is left the residue of the estate would pay them. Certain potential difficult and complex issues can arise for which a solicitor's advice is strongly recommended. Consult a solicitor if any of the following apply:

1 The estate is insufficient to cover debts or to pay all legacies, or has no residue.
2 The will is not clear.
3 The deceased was a partner in a firm or owned his own business.
4 There is a family trust.
5 There may be 'hidden' or unknown debts.
6 The title to the property must be transferred.
7 The will (or intestacy) leaves sizeable property to someone under the age of 18 but does not specify who should act on behalf of the child.
8 The deceased has left no will and is survived by a spouse and children.
  The value of the estate exceeds the threshold under which, according to intestacy rules, it would all go to the spouse. Therefore the part of the estate which exceeds the threshold amount is shared in two ways, as described in chapter eight. This gives the surviving spouse a 'life interest' which requires legal advice.

As explained in chapter eight the threshold concerned in 1990 was £75,000.

---

9 The deceased was part of an insurance syndicate.
10 Agricultural property is involved.
11 There is no will and a 'long-lost' relative is entitled to part of the estate.
12 Someone may seek a share (or larger share) of the estate under the Inheritance (Provision for Family and Dependants) Act.
13 There is any risk that the will may be invalid or it may be suggested that the will is not valid. Consider matters

carefully if the will is on a home-made will form or if there is any doubt in respect of the construction of the terms of the will.

Preparing to value assets

In getting ready to value the deceased's assets, it will be useful to make a provisional list. This should itemize assets and debts so that debts can be deducted from the gross value of the estate to indicate the net value. IHT is then deducted from this figure as are expenses likely to arise in arranging probate. This will at least indicate whether the estate is solvent.

To get more accurate valuations of assets and to get written confirmation, you will need to write to various parties, including the bank, insurance company, mortgage company and so on as appropriate.

The letter to each of these will need to include the following points:

- the full name and date of death of the deceased
- explain you are executor and name any other executors
- enclose the appropriate death certificate
- confirm that an official copy of the death certificate will be sent once the grant of probate is received
- identify the asset in question, the name in which it is held, the reference number and the approximate value
- ask what needs to be done to release the asset to you

Obtaining current figures

Current figures can be obtained from the citizen's advice bureau or inland revenue office

	1990 Figures	Current Rate
1 The threshold over which the inland revenue would require executors to sign an inland revenue account even when probate is not required	£100,000	
2 In the case of a beneficiary being left the deceased's National Savings (bank account savings or money from certain pension funds) the threshold under which a grant may not be required	£5,000	

11   Assets

The house

In dealing with the deceased's estate, it may be necessary to value a house or houses, house contents and cash, assuming of course that these are part of the estate.

A house may be valued by a professional surveyor and valuer. Or an estimate can be made based on the asking prices of similar houses in the district. This estimate will be later checked by the district valuer, an official working for the inland revenue office.

As there are no exact prices for property, the price being subject to supply and demand, it is reasonable to regard a house as having a value band. This would be the range between a rather low valuation and a rather high one. In certain circumstances, a lower valuation could be beneficial and the same applies to a higher valuation.

A lower valuation could save IHT. On the other hand a higher valuation might be preferable if any future sale of the house could incur capital gains tax (CGT). This would be especially worth considering where no IHT is payable on the estate. CGT is worked out using the original value of the house declared for IHT purposes. So where a higher valuation is originally given, the future capital gain and the consequent CGT will be smaller.

In most cases there is exemption from CGT because the house is a private residence. But where this does not apply the higher house valuation for IHT purposes may be worth considering.

On the deceased's death, if any outstanding mortgage is linked with a life insurance policy, the policy will pay off the outstanding mortgage.

Otherwise you will need to find out the extent of any mortgage outstanding. Statements from the bank or building society who originally lent the money will indicate how much remains to be paid at the date of the particular statement.

To get the details of the amount of loan outstanding at the time of the deceased's death, you need to write to the bank or building society concerned. The letter should provide the following information:

1 the name of the deceased and the date of death
2 explain that you are the executor and name any other executors
3 the address of the deceased's house. (Confirm that the deceased was the owner)
4 the reference number of the deceased's mortgage which will help identify the account and the date the mortgage was made
5 the death certificate

It should also ask for the following information:

1 the exact amount of capital still owing at the date of death
2 the amount of interest due up to the date of death

The question can be complicated if the deceased's house was held jointly with another person or several others (joint tenants or tenants-in-common).

If the house is owned by joint tenants the deceased's share goes automatically to the surviving tenant, irrespective of anything the deceased's will might say.

In the case of tenants-in-common, the share of the property that was owned by the deceased becomes part of his estate at death. The deceased's will may give the share to the co-owner or it may not.

If a house is in the joint names of any two people (including a husband and wife) and one dies, the value of the deceased's share must be declared for the purposes of IHT.

So what are the implications of joint property? First of all, if there is any suspicion that a property could be jointly owned, check the deceased's documents carefully and study the title deeds. If mortgage is still owing, these should be held by the bank or building society which arranged the mortgage.

The value of a share in a jointly held house can differ according to whether it was held as tenants-in-common or as joint tenants.

In the case of tenants-in-common, you need to confirm the way in which the property was shared. This will depend on the remaining number of tenants-in-common and whether the property was held in equal shares. These will determine the value of the deceased's share at the date of his death.

Where there are joint tenants, the shares in the property will be equally divided. Clearly where there are two joint tenants the share of the property will be half and half.

The value of the deceased's share of the house for IHT purposes is worked out as follows.

First, the vacant possession value at the date of the deceased's death is calculated. From this overall value, that of the deceased's share is worked out.

Next, a reduction is made in the estimated value of the deceased's share. The percentage of this reduction might be around 15% and may be best estimated by a professional valuer. It arises because the deceased was only a part owner of the property, and by his death leaves the other owner(s) with the right to live there. Therefore the value of the deceased's share cannot be simply the same proportion of the overall vacant possession value that it would be if no one was entitled to live in the property. For IHT purposes, the value of the deceased's portion is estimated as what a buyer would pay in the light of current market values on the date of death, given the fact that another person (or several other people) are still entitled to live there.

Such a reduction in value may be agreed by the valuation officer. For legal reasons, the arrangement cannot be agreed where the joint owners are husband and wife.

If the surviving co-owner is a spouse, the valuation of the deceased's share is taken as half of the vacant possession value. Should the property be in the sole name of the spouse who dies, the surviving spouse may claim that he. or she had their own beneficial share of the property. This could reduce the liability to IHT to the deceased's share of the property only.

The value of the deceased's share of the property is affected if any mortgage is owing. It is reduced by that proportion of the outstanding mortgage that is 'owed' by the deceased's share of the property. For instance, say the deceased owned half of a property and the outstanding mortgage on the whole house was £10,000. The value of the deceased's share would drop by half of this, that is by £5,000.

House contents (including cash)

House contents cover all household effects (including furniture), personal possessions (including clothes), any loose cash, and the car.

If the deceased shared the house with another person, say their spouse, only the deceased's property should be valued for tax purposes.

A husband and wife may have regarded most or all of their property as jointly owned. When one of them dies such property then passes automatically to the other, becoming the survivor's sole property (irrespective of the terms of any will or of intestacy). In this case, only a half of this property needs to be considered for tax purposes.

Not all property may be jointly owned. Some items may be the property of solely one partner. Where items were clearly the sole property of the deceased they must be included in any valuation. Where a husband and wife are involved it is generally taken that items are owned jointly. Where two other people are concerned say an unmarried couple, the assumption is that the purchaser of the item owns it.

Once it is established whether all the household items are to be valued or only some, the task can be started.

Individual items need not be specified when giving an estimate of the value of house contents, but it is easier to itemize items as you value them for the clarity of your own records. The total valuation is then submitted to the capital taxes office of the inland revenue.

More expensive items may be valued by the executors to the best of their ability, although sometimes the valuation of a specialist may be necessary. A jeweller, or an art dealer or a furrier may help with items relevant to their respective spheres, for instance. If such help is called on, it should be made clear to the experts making the valuation that their assessment is for the purposes of probate. This means that the value will be the second-hand value, not the cost of replacement which could well be greater and could increase the amount of IHT due. The specialist valuers should be asked for a certificate of valuation. Their fees can be claimed by the executor as a cost of administering the estate.

The same approach applies to all the items to be valued. It is the second-hand value at the date of death which is estimated, not the replacement value.

Some items may have been being bought on hire-purchase by the deceased and there could be instalments outstanding at the time of death. Such items should be valued, at second-hand value. If the value is relatively small the amount is added to total valuation list. The total of any outstanding instalments should be noted as a debt against the estate.

If the value is relatively large, the item should be valued in the same way but the debt owing should be deducted from the second-hand value leaving net amount to be declared for IHT purposes.

Bank accounts

If the deceased held a current account at a bank in their name only, the executor should inform the appropriate branch of the bank about the death as soon as possible.

Details of the account number, the exact name in which the account was held and the bank's address may be gleaned from any past bank statements found among the deceased's papers.

Any bank cards should be returned to the bank. These might include cheque guarantee cards and cards for cash dispensers.

In writing to the bank to inform them of the death and explain that you are the executor, you will need to include the following information:

1 the exact name in which the current account was held
2 the account number
3 the estimated balance if known

If the deceased had a deposit account at the bank, relevant statements may be found amongst the deceased's papers. Similarly, property such as documents or jewellery may have been deposited and there may be papers indicating this. The will itself may refer to such items. If there is any doubt, write to the bank to check.

Once the bank is informed of the death, they take certain routine steps. Any cheques drawn on the account and still in the pipeline are not honoured. They are returned to the payee with a note stating that the drawer has died. Any money owing to a payee in this way becomes a debt of the estate. If any money was to be paid into the deceased's account, these sums will be temporarily placed in a suspense account by the bank. Any standing orders or direct debits normally paid from the account will cease. Similar procedures are followed if the account is with Girobank.

What happens where the deceased held a joint bank account? The guiding principles are similar to those for any joint assets including building society accounts or savings bank accounts.

First, the executor may need to establish what proportion of the balance belonged to the deceased. This would involve checking who paid the money into the account. These payments may, for example, have been salary cheques or credits from the respective employers of the two account holders.

Joint account holders may have paid their own money

into the account, perhaps from respective bank accounts. Past payments into the joint account over a period of several years may indicate the relevant proportion of the credit balance to be attributed to the deceased.

It is not always possible to calculate the appropriate proportions. For instance, the sources of the payments into the joint account may be numerous. In such cases, it is assumed that an equal share is owned by the joint holders.

Where the joint account holders are husband and wife the situation tends to be simpler. The account is considered to be equally held. Therefore half the balance at the deceased's death is taken to be the deceased's property for IHT purposes. The surviving spouse may continue to use the account as their own and may use the total balance.

Whether or not the joint account holders are husband and wife, the survivor can continue drawing on the account after the other holder has died. The survivor, at the death of the deceased normally becomes the beneficiary of the credit balance of the account. The exception is when the two account holders had previously made some other agreement about it.

The appropriate proportion of the credit balance of a joint account is included in calculating IHT. This is done even where the survivor is a spouse and no IHT will be payable.

The joint account can be used to pay IHT on two conditions. There must be sufficient money in it. The surviving joint-owner of the account must be the residuary beneficiary.

Building society account

If the deceased held an account with a building society, the passbook should show the address of the branch where the account was opened, and the balance (allowing for the possibility that deposits or/and withdrawals may have been made using the hole in the wall dispensing machines).

You should return the passbook to the branch manager so that the death can be noted in the book to effectively protect the account from illegal withdrawals.

A letter to the manager should ask for the final balance once any transactions unknown to you have been processed.

National Savings

Where the deceased held National Savings, the relevant National Savings certificate book(s) should be checked. From the book, you will need the following information:

1 serial number of each certificate
2 date of issue
3 the cost of the certificate
4 the number of units each certificate represents

Get a form, DNS 904 (SB4) from the post office and fill in the necessary information, which will include the information above. The form will ask if any of the savings are held jointly or in trust. It will ask you to confirm that the deceased left a will for which you are executor and for which you intend to get a grant of probate.

You should also specify whether you require the money to be repaid or prefer to keep the assets in National Savings.

Once the form is completed, it is sent to the appropriate address according to the type of savings concerned.

Where several different types of National Savings are concerned, the form should be returned with the security of the savings to the most appropriate address. That office will see that all the different types of National Savings are dealt with including savings certificates and premium bonds.

The various offices dealing with each type of saving would be informed and will send you a valuation of the asset and a repayment form or a transfer form according to your request on the earlier form DNS 904 (SB4).

Before National Savings pay, they may want to see the

grant of probate. This may not be necessary where the savings were nominated, jointly held, held in trust or were £5,000 or less.

Premium savings bonds represent a special case. Although they should be sent with other assets when you send off form DNS 904 (SB4) they will not be officially valued. This is because the interest from them is used to finance the monthly ERNIE lottery draw. The bonds themselves simply keep their face value. They cannot be nominated nor transferred to any beneficiary directly. However, they can be left in the lottery for twelve calendar months following the date of death. They may then be cashed, and the money used by the beneficiary. For the period of one year only from the date of death is the estate entitled to any prize in the draw. After that period the estate is not entitled to any prize and must encash the bonds.

Notify the bonds and stock office as soon as possible of the deceased's death. What happens if a prize is received after the death? This should be sent back to the bonds and stock office. They will then check whether or not the deceased's estate is entitled to the money. What if a prize is paid into the deceased's account after the date of death but before you have been able to contact the bank or the bonds and stock office to report the death? In this case, the prize should be returned as before so that a new prize warrant can be sent to you once you have registered probate.

Any prize won after the date of death is included as part of the total value of National Savings.

Life insurance

If the deceased held life insurance, you need to examine the policy. It may be among documents kept in the deceased's home or it may have been deposited with the bank.

The policy will indicate the insurance company involved and the amount payable at the deceased's death.

You should write to the local branch of the company and include the following information:

1 the full name of the deceased
2 the nature of the insurance, that is, life insurance
3 the date that the policy was issued
4 the policy reference number
5 the value of the policy

If the policy is 'with profits', an extra sum will be added to the assured sum, and you should ask the insurance company to specify the amount.

Stocks and shares

Stock and share certificates may be kept in a safe place in the deceased's home or may be deposited with the bank. You should first make a list of the shares. They are likely to be ones quoted on the International Stock Exchange in London.

It is now necessary to calculate the value of the shares for IHT purposes. The prices of each holding of shares must be noted as they stood at the close of dealing on the day before the deceased died. Two figures will be involved, the selling price (the lower one) and the buying price (the higher one).

If the deceased died at the weekend, prices of the shares may be taken from Friday's or Monday's closing prices. Alternatively you can choose a mixture of Monday's and Friday's prices to give the best price. The relevant figures can be gleaned from one of several sources:

1 Your bank manager
2 A stockbroker
3 The Stock Exchange daily official list

This daily list gives closing prices for the previous day. (Back copies may be bought from the Stock Exchange.) You can collect a copy personally or, for an extra fee, have it posted to you. Alternatively the local reference library may have a copy.

Having found the two closing prices on the appropriate date for the shares you wish to value, find the difference between the two figures, divide it by four and add this to the lower value. This gives the value required. The appropriate value is multiplied by the number of shares held.

To check that all the share holdings have been included, you should next write to the registrar of each company in which the deceased held shares. The appropriate address may be on the dividend warrant counterfoil.

A dividend warrant is effectively a cheque by which a dividend is paid out. It is made out for the amount of the dividend declared by the company. The dividend warrant counterfoil merely shows the amount payable. It should be kept for tax reasons as the counterfoils are normally required by the inland revenue when dealing with the income tax and capital gains tax of a deceased person.

You can also find the address you need in the Register of Registrars held by some reference libraries. Or the company involved will give you the address of the registrar.

Having obtained the correct address, write giving the deceased's full name, the number of shares in the company and your name as executor and listing any other executors.

Request confirmation of the holding and ask if there are any dividends or interest payments not yet claimed. Enclose a copy of the death certificate.

Keep a close record of all replies. The inland revenue must be informed for income tax purposes of any income from securities that may accrue while you are administering the estate.

There is a complication if any of the share prices are quoted 'ex-dividend', denoted by 'xd' beside the closing prices.

With such shares, the company gets dividend cheques ready in advance to send to the owner of the shares. If the shares are sold after the dividend cheques have been prepared, the dividend will still be sent automatically to the original owner. This of course lowers the selling price because both seller and buyer know that the seller will get the dividend. Therefore, for a certain period, the share price is quoted ex-dividend, until the dividends have been issued.

Where the deceased leaves shares which are ex-dividend on the relevant date, the dividend which is due has to be itemized as another asset.

The company registrar will be able to inform you of the dividend due to be paid out on each share. The total dividend due on the shares left by the deceased can then be calculated. From the gross value of the dividend, basic rate income tax is deducted to give the net amount expected. This amount is itemized separately in the deceased's inland revenue account. If the deceased leaves shares which are not quoted on the International Stock Exchange, this raises possible complications. Such shares are recognizable by having Ltd or Limited after the company name rather than PLC or Public Limited Company. Although a valuation from the company accountant may be accepted for probate, it may not. An accountant may then best act on your behalf to agree a value.

The deceased may hold units in a unit trust. A unit trust is a basket of investments chosen to spread the risk of investing and is bought and sold in units of the basket rather than in shares in the individual companies which may comprise the basket. The units are bought from and sold to the unit trust manager rather than on the Stock Exchange.

The value of units when their holder dies is calculated in the same way as for stocks and shares. The closing prices for the day prior to the date of death can be obtained by writing to the trust manager.

Pensions

The deceased may have been receiving a pension before they died. It might have been derived from their own contributions or it might have been a widow's/widower's pension received under a scheme contributed to by the late spouse of the deceased. On the death of the deceased, it may yield a lump sum to the estate.

To establish the conditions of the pension scheme, you should first check the papers held by the deceased. Next, write to the secretary of the pension fund to establish whether the estate is entitled to receive anything under the scheme.

This may be a lump sum or simply an amount due for the last days of the deceased's life. The reply letter should be kept as a record in connection with IHT.

Where a lump sum is payable because contributions paid in by the deceased are returned at his or her death, the sum is declared for IHT.

But many schemes allow for the trustees of the pension fund to choose who receives the money within the regulations of the agreement. The sum may be paid out so as not to attract IHT. It may be paid to the deceased's widow for instance.

If the deceased had been receiving a national insurance retirement pension, executors can claim any arrears plus the pension for the full week in which death occurred.

The deceased's pension book should show the position. The Department of Social Security should be informed of any arrears due and will make the necessary payments to the estate. This will be declared for IHT and noted in probate documents.

Income tax

You should write to the inspector of taxes for the district under which the deceased's tax affairs are dealt with.

The letter should list the deceased's income up to the date of death. This might have inlcuded a salary and a pension. Interest from savings, and dividends from investments would be mentioned. Income already subject to tax should be noted, such as interest on a building society account taxed at source.

It may be that the estate is entitled to a tax rebate. There are several possible reasons for this. The pay as you earn (PAYE) tax system is based on a person's assumed income from 6 April to 5 April, the financial year.

An amount is deducted each month (or week) so that the projected overall amount of tax that will be due over the year is taken out in fairly equal bites.

If someone dies while this process is underway the assumption of earnings for the whole year can be thrown off course, unless the death occurs in say late March, close to the end of the financial year.

Also, some income may be taxed at the standard rate before it is received. Share dividends are an example. Now if the deceased's income did not reach the level at which standard rate tax came into effect, the estate may be entitled to a refund of tax paid on income such as share dividends.

Another point may work in favour of the deceased's tax position. Tax allowances like the married men's personal allowance, are given for the whole year. They remain in force even if the deceased dies early in the financial year. This may also lead to a tax refund.

The inspector of taxes for the appropriate district will write back and may confirm that a rebate may be due. You will need to fill in a tax form.

When the time comes to complete the probate form, the possible tax refund can be estimated. The correct figure, when it is known can be given to the tax office later.

Outstanding social security benefits

Social security benefits may be owing to the deceased. These might include income support, housing benefit or family credit.

If the deceased received any of the above benefits, he or she may be entitled to a payment under the social fund Maternity and Funeral Expenses (General) Regulations 1987. However, any such funeral payment could be recoverable from the deceased's estate by the Department of Health and Social Security.

You should write to the local DSS office or call in for advice on how to claim, taking all relevant documents with you.

12 Total Assets and Debts, and Finance for IHT

Total assets and debts

As replies are received from the holders of the deceased's assets, you will be able to modify your provisional list of estimated values and substitute the exact value of the assets.

As we have seen these may include a house, its contents, car, cash, money in bank or building society accounts, National Savings, premium bonds, life insurance, stocks and shares, outstanding pension money and income tax rebates.

Debts must also be listed. They may include funeral costs, outstanding house mortgage, any hire-purchase payments due, IHT, an estimate of the cost of administering the estate, outstanding bills for gas, electricity, community charge, telephone, overdraft, mail order catalogues, credit card debts, and so on.

The invoices for money owed should be kept carefully and the relevant company, institution, organization or individual contacted. In a short letter, you should explain the situation and agree to pay the creditors after probate has been granted.

We have already noted that, if the estate is insolvent, that is the assets do not clear all the debts, you should call in a solicitor.

In such cases there is a legal order of precedence of creditors as follows:

1 creditors whose loan is secured by a mortgage

2 funeral, testamentary and administrative costs
3 VAT debts

An executor would normally not get involved in the
attempted administration of an insolvent estate. The creditors can take out on their own behalf a grant of letters of
administration in connection with the estate.

Assuming the estate is solvent, debts have to be met.
Mortgaged property may be willed to a beneficiary. If the
will states that this is 'free of any mortgage owing on the
property', then the residuary of the estate will be used to
pay off any outstanding mortgage. If no such stipulation is
made in the will, the beneficiary shoulders the debt of
outstanding mortgage.

The mortgage company, bank or building society concerned can demand repayment of the outstanding mortgage from the beneficiary. Alternatively it can ask for the
property to be sold to clear the debt.

A similar situation arises if the property is part of the
residuary estate and is not specifically itemized in the will.
The residuary beneficiary is in debt to the creditor in a
similar way.

With the exception of such mortgaged property, debts
are normally paid out of the residuary. What if there is not
enough in the residuary? Then all the pecuniary legacies
have to be reduced in proportion until outstanding debts
are met. If the pecuniary legacies still leave debts
uncovered then other property left by the will is propor-
tionately reduced until debts are cleared.

In Scotland, particular caution must be exercized if the
executor sees that the estate is insolvent. He must cease
administering the estate and immediately petition the court
for sequestration.

If he fails to comply, he may be held personally liable for
the debts.

Finance for IHT

IHT has to be paid before a grant of probate can be
obtained. The probate will allow the bank or building

society or other holder of the deceased's assets to release the asset. But until the assets are released, there is difficulty in paying IHT. How do you cut through this Gordian knot?

National Savings can be called on if funds are not available from any other source. The deceased may hold National Savings certificates, premium bonds, British savings bonds, money paid in through a SAYE (save as you earn) agreement, or government stocks on the National Savings stock register and which are kept by National Savings. Such funds can be used to finance IHT payment.

When you initially visit the probate registry, you explain that you wish to use National Savings as finance for IHT.

Staff at the probate registry will then give you a note. This will confirm that a personal application has been made and will specify the amount of IHT due and the probate fees to be paid.

The probate registry staff will then send this note to the relevant National Savings office. You will have already sent the proofs of ownership for each of the types of National Savings with your form DN 5904. You will have received back from National Savings confirmation of the value of the assets.

After National Savings receive the note from the Probate Registry, they will send a cheque for the total value of IHT and probate fees to the Registry.

Once probate is obtained, the remaining money in National Savings is accessible to you.

However, if the assets include the balance of pay-as-you-earn money or yearly plan money, this will earn no more interest. It will simply be repaid when the grant of probate is presented.

A building society account that was held by the deceased may be used to pay IHT and probate fees, with the society's agreement. They will make out a cheque for IHT to the inland revenue and one for probate fees to the Paymaster General.

The deceased might have a Girobank account. If the estate is solvent, you may be able to borrow money from the account up to the limit of the balance in the account, to pay IHT.

The money could be raised by a temporary bank loan.

The amount of the loan would have to be sufficient to comfortably cover IHT and probate fees. A loan account could be opened. Another account may then be opened for the use of the executor(s) and a cheque book allocated for use with the account. Cheques would then be written as necessary for IHT and probate fees.

You should arrange with the bank that these payments are made clearly distinguishable from other withdrawals from the special account. This means that (by agreement with the bank) the interest due can be deducted from the estate's income for income tax purposes. This arrangement holds during the administration of the estate.

Once probate is obtained, you can then transfer the money in the deceased's own account to the executor's account. This would cut down the balance of the loan and hence the interest. As the assets of the estate come in the loan is cleared.

There are two ways in which money can sometimes be saved.

You can ask the bank manager, if he will consider the deceased's account and the loan account as one. In this way money previously owned by the deceased is set off against the loan in the executor's account thus reducing the interest.

Another method is to ask the manager to place any balance in the deceased's current account into a deposit account still in the deceased's name where it will earn interest. Any interest accrued in this way would be declared on the income tax return for the duration of the administration of the estate.

13   Probate Registries, Probate Forms and the Grant

Controlling probate registries

You do not have to wait for all the replies to come back from the holders of the deceased's assets before sending for probate forms.

In determining the most convenient place to write to for the forms, it is worth remembering that you will have to visit a registry or one of its local offices at least once in the process of obtaining a grant of probate.

A list of controlling probate registries is given at the end of the book. If it would be convenient for you to visit one of these at a later date, then you should telephone or write to that registry asking for probate papers. These registries are open between 9.30 a.m. and 4 p.m. Monday to Friday.

Local offices

It may be however, that none of the controlling registries are conveniently situated near you. In this case, it is better to choose a local office with your future visit in mind.

It is important, however, to note that some local offices open quite infrequently, perhaps only once a month. This may delay your access to the grant of probate.

A list of local offices, their opening times and the appropriate controlling probate registry will be sent to you by the probate registry.

If having checked the list, it appears that a local office would be more convenient for you, make a note of its controlling probate registry.

You should then write to the controlling probate registry or telephone them for the probate forms. Do not write to the local office. Because they open infrequently, this could well seriously delay your application.

Forms for information

The probate registry will send the following for information:

1 A booklet 'How to obtain probate – A Guide for the Applicant Acting Without a Solicitor' (form PA2). This briefly covers some of the matters we are considering, including the nature of probate, the grant of representation and applying for a grant and duty and tax. The booklet also lists the controlling probate registries and their respective local offices.
2 A list of 'Local Offices – addresses and opening times'. (Form PA3).
3 'Fees payable by a personal applicant' (form PA4). This refers to probate fees which are set on a sliding scale according to the net value of the estate. The table provided by the probate registry is intended only as a guide, the exact sum being confirmed when you are later called for interview at the local office of your choice. No money is paid for probate fees until the interview confirms the appropriate amount.

The fees may vary from time to time. The fees current in 1990 are given below, simply to give an idea of the sliding scale of fees. The current fees should be checked when you receive the latest issue of form PA4.

Probate fees on Net Estates

Net estate (£)	Probate fee
0 – 500	£ 1.00
501 – 1,000	£2.00
1,001 – 5,000	£5.00
5,001 – 6,000	£6.00
6,001 – 7,000	£7.00
7,001 – 8,000	£8.00
8,001 – 9,000	£9.00
9,001 – 10,000	£10.00
10,001 – 25,000	£40.00 **plus** £1.00 for every £1,000 or part of £1,000
25,001 – 40,000	£80.00 **plus** £1.00 for every £1,000 or part of £1,000
40,001 – 70,000	£150 **plus** £1.00 for every £1,000 or part of £1,000
70,000 – 100,000	£3.50 for every £1,000 or part of £1,000
OVER 100,000	£250.00 for the first £100,000 and £50.00 for every additional £100,000 or part of £100,000 **plus** £1.00 for every £1,000 or part of £1,000

The net estate is the declared value of the estate for the purpose of IHT. It does not include any part of the estate which passes by survivorship.

Survivorship may be explained by giving an example. Suppose a man and his wife own property, say a house, which is in their joint names beneficially and not as tenants-in-common in any form of definite shares (for example, equal shares). On the death of one partner the property will pass to the survivor. No grant will be required for that particular property as it passes automatically to the survivor of beneficial joint tenants. In the case of property, all that one need do is put a copy of the death certificate with the deeds.

The figures for 1990 may be taken as an example.

The fee due for a net estate of up to £10,000 are straightforward, being simply a flat sum.

The fees for estates valued higher than £10,000 are not as complicated to calculate as first appears.

For example, if the estate is £42,300 it falls within the net estate band of £40,001 – £70,000 in the table. There is therefore a flat fee of £150 plus £1 for every £1,000 or part of £1,000 of the estate's value. On an estate of £42,300, the fee is £150 plus £43 (£42 for the £42,000 plus £1 for the £300 which counts as part of a £1,000). The probate fee totals £193.

If the estate had a net value of £80,500, this would fall within the band of £70,001 – £100,000. For this band there is no flat fee but simply a payment of £3.50 for every £1,000 or part of £1,000 of the net estate. The calculation is therefore $81 \times £3.50 = £283.50$.

Should the net estate be for instance £180,000, this comes in the 'over £100,000' bracket. The fee is calculated by totalling the following:

		£
1	£250 for the first £100,000	= 250
2	£50 for every additional £100,000 or part of £100,000	= 50
3	£1 for every £1,000 or part of £1,000	= 180
		£480

The fee is paid for the service given by the probate registry of handling the necessary papers and eventually giving a grant of probate. When you are called to the registry to swear the papers, the fee must be paid.

If paying by cheque, it is made payable to HM Paymaster General, and the fee is of course chargeable to the estate. Indeed, if you have arranged with the bank to open an executor account, with a temporary arrangement for an overdraft, the cheque would be drawn from that.

When you eventually visit the registry, you should also get several official copies of the probate for which there is a small charge. Each of these will be sent to the various people who hold the deceased's assets to show them that probate has been granted. Such people or organizations might include the deceased's bank, building society and insurance company.

Forms for completion

As well as the forms for information, the probate registry will send the following forms for completion:

1 Probate Application Form (PA1)
2 Spouse's Contributions Form (PA5)
3 Statement of Stocks and Shares etc (Cap form 40)
4 Schedule of Real and Leasehold/Immovable Property (Cap form 37B)
5 A Return of the Whole Estate (Cap form 44)

If all goes smoothly, you fill in the forms as necessary and return them by post or by hand at the proper opening times. Registry staff then check the forms and assess IHT and probate fees due.

Using the information you provide as a basis, they then prepare a document and write to you giving an appointment date and time. At the specified time, you and any other executors should personally visit the registry to swear the document to be true.

Each of the five forms mentioned above will now be considered in detail.

Probate application form (PA1)

The probate application form comprises 5 sections:

1 This asks at which probate registry or local office you want to be interviewed. This may be the registry which has sent you the forms or one of its local offices.
2 Details required include name, address, occupation, legal marital status, date of birth, date of death and age of the deceased.
3 You are asked if the deceased left a will, if anyone under eighteen years old receives a gift in the will, and if there are any executors named in the will.

   Also you have to give the name(s) of any executors who are not applying. Beside each name you insert a key letter A, B, C or D. These represent the reason the particular executor is not applying.

   A = died before the deceased
   B = died after the deceased
   C = does not wish to apply
   D = does not wish to apply now but may later

   If an executor does not apply for reason 'D', then the registry will send a 'power reserved' letter which that executor may sign. Should any of the acting executors be unable to continue their task, the previously non-acting executor may then take over. An acting executor may die for instance before his or her duties are completed.
4 This concerns relatives that survived the deceased, that is were alive when the deceased died. It also covers certain relatives who did not survive the deceased. In each case, you have to enter the number of relatives concerned in one of two boxes according to whether they were under or over eighteen years old.

   You are also asked whether the deceased or any of his or her relatives were adopted.
5 You are required to enter routine details about yourself including name, address, occupation and marital status. You are asked if you are related to the deceased and if so

what that relationship is in law. The name and address of any surviving spouse must be given unless you are yourself that spouse.

Finally, you give the details of any other applicants, that is your fellow executors. Their full names and addresses should be given.

The form mentions that the grant will normally be sent to the first applicant.

When returning the form, the following must also be enclosed:

1 the death certificate
2 the original will (if one exists)
3 form Cap 44 'A Return of the Whole Estate'

A photocopy of the will should be taken and kept in a safe place before the original is sent. No document or anything else should be attached to the will.

Spouse's contributions (PA5)

The title of this single sheet form is tucked away unhelpfully in the bottom left hand corner. The heading states:

'Complete this form if:
the deceased left a surviving husband or wife and there is a matrimonial home in the SOLE name of the deceased.'

The form seeks to establish whether or not a surviving spouse is entitled to a share or interest in the house and if so what percentage of its value this should be. It is important to establish this if the deceased's will did not allocate the property to the surviving spouse.

The information is also relevant even if the deceased has willed all or part of the property to his or her spouse. This is because, apart from stipulations in the will, the spouse may have a share of or interest in the property in their own right. The value of the deceased's estate may therefore be affected. The forms asks:

'Was there any written agreement about the house being jointly owned by husband and wife?'

If this is the case, simply attach the written agreement to the form and sign the form, leaving the remaining questions.

If there is no such written agreement, the form goes on to ask if the surviving spouse wishes:

'to claim that he or she acquired an interest because he or she made substantial financial contributions towards the purchase of the house of earnings or savings'.

If no such interest is claimed, you say so and simply sign the form. If an interest is claimed, you are asked for 'details of how the contribution was able to be made'.

Here details of contributions towards purchasing the property are given. The spouse may wish to claim an interest because he or she paid towards the renovation or extension of the property.

Finally the form asks:

'What percentage of the value of the house (at the date of death of the deceased) does the surviving husband or wife claim to have acquired?'

This may later have to be agreed with the district valuer or with any other person who acquired the interest of the property.

Statement of stocks and shares etc (Cap 40)

This form is divided into seven columns, the seventh being for official use. The other six columns require the following information:

Column 1 – name of company etc

Write the name of the company followed by a full description of the class of share or stock. This information can be found on the certificates themselves. If you know the company registration number this should be included. You are also asked to specify if any of the items are 'bearer' shares. In the case of bearer shares, no specific owner's name is shown on the certificate and they are owned by whoever has rightful possession of the certificate.

The form asks you to list items in a particular order. First of all, securities quoted on the Stock Exchange should be listed in the order in which they appear in the official lists. Secondly, securities quoted on any other recognized stock exchange are entered. Finally, other items are listed. They may include shares in companies not quoted on the Stock Exchange. The form asks you to total such items separately from the total of all the other stocks and shares.

Any shares which were ex-dividend at the date of death should be identified by putting 'xd' after the name of the shares.

Column 2 – unit of quotation

This is the unit of the stock or shares whose value was quoted on the Stock Exchange. Stock is often quoted in £1 units, shares are usually quoted per individual share. Unit trusts would be entered as 'one unit'.

Column 3 – holding number of shares or amount of stock

This is the number of quoted units held in shares or stock.

Column 4 – market price at date of valuation

This is the value that was obtained using the procedure outlined in the chapter on assets under the headings of stocks and shares, pensions and income tax. The form reminds us of this procedure, stating:

'Prices based upon published quotations should normally be taken at ¼ up from the lower to the higher limit of quotation.'

Column 5 – sources of market price if other than the Stock Exchange official list for date of valuation

We will assume that the official list was used for valuation. If the date of valuation was a day on which no quotations were available (say a weekend) you will remember that the price based on the list for the latest previous date or earliest subsequent date may be used. If a 'mix' of the two lists are used, you might enter the date of the relevant list in this column, crossing out the column heading and appending a note to explain.

Column 6 – principal value at date of valuation

This is the number of shares or the amount of stock multiplied by the market price at the date of valuation.

In the case of ex-dividend shares you will not have received the dividend warrant. You should, however, have informed the company of the deceased's death and of your being executor. The dividend warrant would be then sent to you after you had obtained probate and given the company evidence of this.

Even though you have no dividend warrant, you will know the dividend declared and this should be entered. The dividend per share declared at the date of the deceased's death should be multiplied by the number of shares to give the total dividend.

Further copies of Cap form 40 can be obtained from the capital taxes office.

Schedule of real and leasehold/immoveable property (Cap 37B)

Separate copies of Cap form 37B should be used for properties in:

1 England and Wales
2 Scotland
3 Northern Ireland
4 Outside the United Kingdom

Extra copies can be obtained from the capital tax office of your country of residence. There are six columns on the form.

Column 1

Simply list the item number 1, 2, 3 etc, remembering that the form concerns various types of property.

Column 2

The description of the property is entered. In the case of a house, its full address would be given.

Column 3

Details of tenure are entered, for instance, in the case of a house you should state whether it was freehold or leasehold. In the case of a long lease, the house has a capital value and this will be entered later in column 6. However, if the deceased was the tenant of a house, the house would have no capital value as far as the deceased is concerned. Such property would not be mentioned on probate forms.

Column 4

This concerns any details of lettings. Tenant's name, period of tenancy, rental, and landlord's outgoings are included.

Column 5

This concerns agricultural land. Where this is involved, professional advice should be sought.

Column 6

The value of property transferred is entered in this column, ignoring reliefs.

In the case of a house where mortgage was still owing, the full capital value on the open market at the date of death is estimated. Any mortgage owing is detailed on other forms and is considered a separate debt for IHT purposes. If a husband or wife is claiming a share in a property which was in the sole name of the deceased spouse, the *full* value of the property should be entered. 'see form PA5' should be written beside the value. The probate registry and inland revenue may then later adjust the figure. At the bottom of the form there are more questions. One concerns timber, and asks if there is timber on the properties and further supplementary items if the answer is yes.

Another asks you to indicate any items whose value had been agreed with the district valuer.

Yet another asks for details of any items which have been sold, including the date of completion of the sale.

A return of the whole estate (Cap 44)

Introduction

Cap 44 is an eight-page form for recording the deceased's assets and debts.

The probate registry may need to use it to prepare the inland revenue account, a document which the personal representatives must sign. If the gross value of the estate falls below a certain threshold, there is no need for an inland revenue account. However, Cap 44 still has to be filled in. The threshold in 1990 for example was £70,000 but the probate registry will inform you of the current figure.

The layout of the form is in three main parts.

Section 1 (pages 1 to 4)
Assets of the deceased in the United Kingdom

Schedule of assets in the United Kingdom
Schedule of debts due to persons resident in the United Kingdom

Section 2 (page 5)
Assets of the deceased outside the United Kingdom

Section 3
Questions relating to property inside and outside the United Kingdom

Each part will now be considered in turn.

Section 1

The first part of this section comprises a schedule of assets in the United Kingdom and is divided into fifteen items.

Item 1 asks for details of the deceased's cash other than money in the bank. As executor, you can use such loose cash for small administration expenses like postage. A record should be kept of outgoings and receipts obtained where appropriate.

Item 2 deals with the deceased's bank account(s). If there are several accounts, for example, a current account, a deposit account and a high interest account, each should be listed along with the appropriate balances and the branch at which the accounts are held.

In the case of deposit and high interest accounts, you should note any interest accumulated but not added to the account. This may arise for example, where interest is normally calculated and credited periodically, say twice yearly.

Item 3 is about money at savings banks, or in building, co-operative or friendly societies, including interest due at the date of death.

Item 4 concerns household and personal goods and would include such items as the car and jewellery valued at best possible price.

Item 5 asks for a list of securities and their gross value at the date of death. These will include British savings bonds, national development bonds, local government bonds, war loans and other government and municipal securities. These may be valued from the Stock Exchange daily official list. Defence bonds are simply worth their face value.

Item 6 requires information on savings certificates and the relevant value should be entered. The letter received from National Savings when you sent them the security for the savings should be attached to the form. Make a note of the reference number of the letter because you will need to quote this when probate is granted and you cash in the savings certificates.

Item 7 is about premium bonds

Item 8 concerns other stocks, shares or investments including unit trusts. This item is covered by Cap 40 – schedule of stocks and shares on which you will have listed these items. The total value of all stocks and shares should be inserted here.

Item 9(a) deals with the deceased's life-insurance policy, if applicable.

Item 9(b) concerns insurance policies taken out by the deceased on another person's life, that person having survived the deceased. Policies under 9(b) constitute assets to the estate. The value of such a policy is its surrender value at the date of the deceased's death. The insurance company will provide this information for you.

Item 10 asks for details about any money due from employers. This includes amounts owing if the deceased was in employment at the time of death. Unpaid wages would come under this remit. Also, other benefits due to the deceased should be noted, such as any superannuation payments.

Item 11 deals with 'reversions'. These are interests which the deceased had in other assets which will not be realized until the death of the benefactor. Reversions may not be subject to tax as part of the deceased person's estate.

Item 12 concerns other assets not itemized elsewhere on the form. Read the form up to the end of page three before you decide if there is anything not included which needs to go under item 12.

Such assets might include an estimate of any money due as a tax refund from the inland revenue, and any money owed to the estate from a state retirement pension not collected by the deceased.

The dividend on any ex-dividend shares would be mentioned, as already calculated on form Cap 40.

Item 13 is applicable only if the deceased was a permanent civil servant at the time of death. A sum would then be paid to the estate known as the civil servants death benefit.

Item 14 is to do with business assets. It is subdivided into:
(a) debts, stock in trade, goodwill, and other business assets
(b) net value of the deceased's interest as a partner in a firm.

If this item 14 applies, then professional advice should be sought.

Item 15 concerns freehold and leasehold property. If the house where the deceased lived was owned solely by him or her, the total value is entered. However, if the deceased was a tenant-in-common, the value of the deceased's portion is entered. The form points out that form Cap 37 should also be completed.

The second part of section 1 covers page four of the form and is a schedule of debts due to persons resident in the United Kingdom. There are four items:

Item 1 asks for information on funeral expenses which the account from the funeral director will show.

Item 2 concerns other debts, such as outstanding bills for

electricity, telephone, and so on, which should be listed.

Item 3 deals with mortgages. The information required is the address of the property on which there is an outstanding mortgage, details of the bank or building society who were owed the money, the date the mortgage was taken out, and the amount outstanding at the date of death.

If the deceased owned the whole property, the complete amount owed is entered. If the deceased had jointly owned the property, the proportion of mortgage owed is entered.

If a policy such as a life assurance policy is linked with the mortgage so that it clears the mortgage when the house owner dies, details must be given. Should the policy be payable to the estate, it is included in IHT calculations.

Item 4 covers information on any business debts which the deceased may have incurred.

Section 2

In this section, which occupies only the top half of page five of the form, there are no numbered items, just two headings. The first asks for particulars of assets and their gross value at the date of death.

The second heading is a schedule of the deceased's debts due to persons resident outside the United Kingdom. The name and address of the persons or companies owed the debt is entered, a description of the debt and the amount involved. The various debts are then totalled, transferred to a box in the particulars of the assets section, and deducted from that amount to give a net total.

All amounts have to be given in sterling using the exchange rate at the date of death.

Section 3

The final part of the form, extending from the foot of page five to page eight, comprises five main items.

Item 1 asks for details of joint assets including any joint foreign assets. Part (a) of the item asks if the deceased was the joint owner of a house or any other freehold or leasehold property. If the answer is 'yes', the form asks for further details in subsections 1 to 5.

These aim to establish the address of the property and the name(s) of the other joint owner(s). If the property was bought in the joint name(s), you are asked to state the date of purchase and to say who provided the purchase money and in what proportion they provided it. You are also asked for details of the deceased's share of the property and its value at the date of death.

The proportions in which the purchase money was provided will influence the shares in the ownership of the property at the date of the deceased's death.

However, if husband and wife are the only joint owners it is generally taken that they owned equal shares of the property.

The property may have been held by two people (not husband and wife) as tenants-in-common. If so, you could argue that the value of the deceased's share on the open market is less than it would have been if the property was with vacant possession. In answer to the question about the deceased's share and its value at the date of death you would mention this and enter the amended value.

You are asked on the form whether the deceased's share accrued by survivorship to the other joint owner(s) or whether it passed under his/her will or intestacy.

'Survivorship' means in this case 'joint tenants'. If the deceased's share passed under the will or intestacy (owned as tenants-in-common) you must include it elsewhere on the form. If a United Kingdom asset, it is entered in item 15 on page three. If a foreign asset, it would go in section 2, (assets of the deceased outside the United Kingdom) on page five.

Item 1(b) asks if the deceased was the joint holder of any savings bank account, other bank accounts, building society accounts, or the owner of savings certificates, investments or other assets. If the answer is yes there are a series of subsections to be dealt with. These are to establish the contributions and withdrawals of each of the joint owners in order to determine the deceased's share.

Matters are simplified if it can be demonstrated that the joint owners intended the property to be equally owned. Also in the case of a husband and wife it is assumed that the property is equally owned.

Item 2 concerns nominated assets. It asks if the deceased in their lifetime nominated any savings bank account, savings, certificates or other money in favour of any person. Assets left under the will are excluded.

Nominated assets must be declared for IHT purposes. They do not however form part of the dealings of the personal representatives but pass directly to the person nominated.

Item 3 relates to gifts and other transfers made by the deceased in their lifetime. These include money and stocks and shares.

This information influences the position on the IHT scale at which the rates start. It affects the calculation of the amount of tax due at the deceased's death.

Certain gifts are exempt and these are listed on the form.

For instance the situation in 1990 is that gifts not totalling more than £3,000 in any one year to 5 April are exempt. But for gifts given before 6 April 1976 the exemption limit was £1,000 for any one year. For gifts betwen 6 April 1976 and 5 April 1981 inclusive, the corresponding limit was £2,000.

The questions to be completed for item 3 begin on page seven of the form. You are asked if, apart from exempted gifts, the deceased made any other gifts within ten years of his or her death. In fact, the regulations have changed since the form was printed and only gifts made within *seven* years of the death need be specified.

3(a) simply asks if the deceased made any gift.

3(b) is concerned with whether the deceased created any

settlement. A settlement is a gift in which the property must be held on trust for the benefit of others.

3(c) asks if the deceased paid any premium on 'a life insurance policy not included in this form'. In the context of gifts, this means any premium which the deceased paid on a life insurance policy for the benefit of someone else.

3(d) asks if the deceased made 'any other transfer of value'. A sale at the full market price to a non-relative is excluded. The term transfer of value refers to the transfer or sale of property at below its full market value. That proportion that was, so to speak, cut off the market value would be considered a kind of gift, except where it came within the exemptions explained in the preamble to item 3.

Whilst a sale at the full market price to a non-relative need not be declared, a sale, even at full market price, to a relative must be entered.

A relative is defined as follows:
 (i) the deceased's spouse, parent, child, uncle or aunt
 (ii) the issue of any relative mentioned in (i).
(iii) the spouse of any relative mentioned in (i) or (ii).

If any gifts were given under any of the headings 3(a), 3(b), 3(c) or 3(d) you are required to specify the date of the gift or disposition and the name and address of those to whom the gift was given (the 'donees'). A description of the asset and its value at the date of transfer must be supplied.

The form advises you that if a full report has already been made to an inland revenue office you need only specify which office was involved and quote any relevant official reference. This would be the case if the deceased had made a large gift in his or her lifetime requiring a tax return to be completed to determine any lifetime tax due.

Item 4 deals with assets held in trust.

4(a) asks if the deceased, during his or her lifetime, was entitled to any benefit in any asset(s) held under a settlement.

A settlement involves someone transferring some of

their property to trustees. The trustees then pay income from the property to another person and at a later time divide up the capital among others. The income from the property may be paid for the lifetime of the person benefiting. Then at his or her death the capital may be divided.

Such a settlement may involve a trust created by deed during the benefactor's life. Or the trust may be created by the benefactor's will at his death or by his dying intestate.

4(b) asks if the deceased was no longer entitled to the above benefits within ten years of death. Details of any such dispositions of property have to be given.

Item 5 deals with superannuation benefits. If a sum of money or annuity becomes payable on the deceased's death under a superannuation scheme, you are asked to state this and attach a letter (or copy) confirming this. The letter will be from the managers or trustees of the scheme setting out details of the benefit payable.

Getting the grant

Some weeks after completing and returning the appropriate probate forms, the controlling probate registry will invite you and any other executor(s) for interview. This will take place at the registry itself or at one of its local offices, if you have requested this.

One of the purposes of the interview is to enable you to check that the forms you will be required to sign are accurate. These forms will be based on the information you have given in the probate forms.

You should therefore take with you all pertinent documents, letters and so on that may help you do this.

At the registry or local office a commissioner will see you, and ask you to check and sign the oath. You will then be required to swear on the bible (or affirm if a non-Christian) that the information you have given is true to the best of your knowledge. The commissioner will also help with any queries you may have.

If there was no will, you would not be applying for a grant of probate, but for a grant of letters of administration. The deceased may have left a will which appointed no executors. Or the executors appointed may not be able or willing to apply for a grant. If you become a personal representative in these circumstances, the grant you get is called 'letters of administration with the will annexed'.

Once these formalities are attended to, you pay the probate fees and order and pay for official copies of the grant. Later, you send each of these to those people who are holding the deceased's assets (bank, building society, etc) so that they can release the assets to you. The official copies are sometimes called sealed copies because they have an impress of the court's seal on them to indicate authenticity.

The grant will be posted to you subsequently, but before that any IHT due has to be dealt with.

The probate office will send you notification that IHT is due and a cheque for the amount should be made out to the inland revenue. The tax is calculated on the net estate in the way that was explained in the chapter on IHT.

An instalment option is possible in certain circumstances when paying IHT. We have already seen that IHT normally has to be paid before the assets of the estate are released, often necessitating a loan which will be repaid from the estate later.

But IHT can be paid in ten yearly instalments for the following:

- houses
- buildings
- land
- a family business
- certain unquoted shares

If at any time during the ten years, the asset is sold, the whole of the outstanding tax becomes due.

Now interest is charged (in 1990 it was 6% per year) on any IHT outstanding from the end of the sixth month after death.

By choosing the instalment option, payment can be delayed on most of the IHT until after the grant is obtained. This saves paying interest on a larger loan which may be much higher than the interest charged on outstanding IHT.

How is the amount due calculated if an instalment option is taken? First of all, IHT is worked out as described in an earlier chapter. If that amount were due on the whole net estate it would simply be paid in full. But it is not going to be paid on the whole net estate, only on a proportion calculated as followed:

$$\frac{\text{net estate minus property with the instalments option}}{\text{net estate}} \times \begin{array}{l}\text{total tax that}\\\text{would have been}\\\text{payable on the}\\\text{whole net estate}\end{array}$$

After payment of the IHT, the grant will be posted to you, possibly some weeks later. Any official copies of the will which you ordered will also be included, the original will being retained for Somerset House, London.

Advertising for creditors

If you have any doubt about whether all the deceased's debts have come to light, you should advertise for creditors once the grant has been issued.

Professional advice should be sought, but essentially, an advertisement should be placed in the *London Gazette* and in a local newspaper. This advertisement states that all claims against the estate have to be made by a certain date. This date cannot be less than two months from the appearance of the announcement.

The reason that professional advice is important is that there is a correct form for the advertisement which must be followed. This then absolves the personal representative from liability to any claims which may be made after the expiry date against the deceased's estate.

Should an advertisement be necessary, you would have to wait until the expiry date had passed before proceeding. (This announcement is known to solicitors as a section 27 notice.)

A note on probate flow diagram

Let us assume that after the death of the deceased, all the funeral formalities have been dealt with. If the deceased had left a will, then his wishes regarding funeral, donation of body or organs will have been taken into account.

You have been named as executor in the will. If there was no will or there was a will but it did not name a personal representative, you are to be administrator.

You decide to take on the responsibilities. What are the steps to follow to get the grant?

The various stages are set out in the flow diagram that follows.

Obtaining the grant of probate/administration

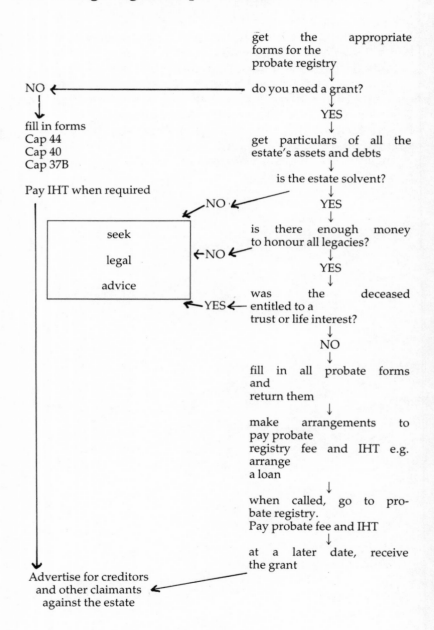

get the appropriate forms for the
probate registry
↓
NO ← do you need a grant?
| ↓
↓   YES
fill in forms   ↓
Cap 44   get particulars of all the
Cap 40   estate's assets and debts
Cap 37B   ↓
                    is the estate solvent?
Pay IHT when required   ↓
                 NO ←   YES
                              ↓
    seek   is there enough money
                  to honour all legacies?
    legal   ←NO ←   ↓
                           YES
    advice   ↓
              ←YES← was the deceased
                    entitled to a
                    trust or life interest?
                              ↓
                             NO
                              ↓
                    fill in all probate forms
                    and
                    return them
                              ↓
                    make arrangements to
                    pay probate
                    registry fee and IHT e.g.
                    arrange
                    a loan
                              ↓
                    when called, go to pro-
                    bate registry.
                    Pay probate fee and IHT
                              ↓
                    at a later date, receive
                    the grant

Advertise for creditors
and other claimants ←
against the estate

14   Further Administering the Estate

Sending an official copy of the grant to asset holders

Once the grant is received, along with a sufficient number of sealed copies, you can send a copy to the deceased's bank and to each of the companies or bodies holding the deceased's assets so they can be released to you.

The sort of letter that might be written to the bank if you have opened an executorship account is as follows:

300 Earl Street
Manchester

10 June 19—

The Manager
Savewell Bank
Grange Road
Manchester

Dear Sir

Re: Arthur John Daniels – deceased

I am now pleased to enclose an office copy of the grant of letters of administration of the probate relating to Arthur John Daniels.

Would you now close the deceased's current account number 123456 and transfer the money into my executor's account number 654321 which I opened on 8th April 19—.

Please return the office copy grant to me at your earliest convenience.

Yours faithfully

Mary King

The holders of assets may include those listed below and the list may be used (and extended) to keep a record of your correspondence with those asset holders.

Asset Holder	Date Copy of Grant Sent to Asset holder	Date Asset Released	Amount of Asset
Bank			
Insurance company			
Inland revenue (tax refund)			
Department of Social Security (arrears of state pension)			
Building society			
National Savings Bank account			
Premium bonds			
Savings certificates*			
Dividend on ex-dividend shares			
Employer's pension			
Outstanding state benefit			

* When sending the grant to National Savings, enclose the application forms for the different assets which you obtained from them when you previously asked for the valuation of the assets.

When any premium bonds are returned, note that they are not transferred and will have to be paid.

In the case of some National Savings, there is an upper limit to the amount any one person can hold. Where National Savings inherited from the deceased push the existing savings of the beneficiary above the upper limit, this is not considered an excess but is allowed.

300 East Street
Manchester

The Manager   12 June 19—
Save and Prosper Building Society
Central Avenue
Manchester

Dear Sir

Re: Arthur John Daniels – deceased

I wrote to you on [*insert date*] informing you of the death of Arthur John Daniels, and asked if you could supply me with details of the assets you hold in his name.

You provided this information in your letter dated [*insert date*] [*give letter reference*].

I now enclose a sealed copy of the grant of probate of the will/letters of administration.

Please could you now send me what is due to the estate and return the sealed copy of the grant once you have registered it.

Yours faithfully

Mary King

Clearing the loan for IHT and probate payments

Assume that you have taken out a loan to cover the costs of IHT and probate fees. Naturally, there will be interest charges on the loan, so it is serving the estate best to pay off both capital and interest as soon as sufficient funds have been released to the estate.

If you have opened an executorship account, you can write to the bank instructing them to transfer sufficient funds from it to clear the loan account.

The loan interest can be deducted from any income tax due from the estate.

Form Cap 30

The IHT payment you have made may need adjusting, and a further payment may have to be made. This arises if you have not reached an agreement with the district valuer about the value of the deceased's house before you paid IHT.

The district valuer will then value the house after IHT has been paid and probate obtained. He may disagree with the valuation you have placed on the house and may, after discussing the matter with you, reach an agreement with you on a higher valuation.

This means that you will not have paid sufficient IHT. The extra amount due is calculated from the increase in value agreed with the district valuer. If the house's new valuation is say £5,000 more than the original valuation, then IHT would be due on that £5,000 at the appropriate rate. If the rate were 40% the tax due would be £2,000 for instance.

If you had arranged to pay the IHT (due on the house) by ten instalments, then any 'extra' IHT due because of increased valuation can be paid with the instalments.

There are other ways in which extra IHT may become due. Assets may be discovered which were not known of when the grant was applied for. Your estimate of an asset may be lower than actually proves to be the case when the asset is released. This may arise where estimates of an income tax refund are involved. In such cases the capital taxes office should be informed. They may require you to sign a corrective document.

The opposite situation occurs sometimes. You may have paid IHT on the calculation of certain assets and debts of the estate, only to discover later that an asset was valued too highly or that a new debt has arisen. In this case, less IHT may be due than the amount which you have in fact paid. You would then contact the capital taxes office to request a refund.

Copies of form Cap 30 are obtained from the inland revenue capital taxes office. Once they are completed satisfactorily and returned, the inland revenue will send you a certificate to confirm that all IHT has been paid on the assets disclosed.

Of course, if the tax due on the deceased's house is to be paid by ten annual instalments, the certificate will not be issued until the final instalment is paid.

Two copies of Cap 30 are completed and returned to the capital taxes office. They will return one copy to you with the certificate confirming that the capital taxes office accept that IHT has been paid on the assets disclosed.

The form is printed on both sides of an A4 sheet and comprises six sections from A to F.

Section A concerns liability arising on death. Section B covers liability in respect of a lifetime transfer and section C involves liability in respect of a settlement without an interest in possession.

The relevant section for our purposes is section A and the word 'none' should be written in sections B and C. In section A you give the deceased person's full name, date of death and the 'title' under which liability arises. This title might be 'will of deceased'. Finally, state the beneficiaries who are entitled to the assets, for example 'legatees under the will'.

Section D deals with 'the property or value transferred in respect of which this application is made' and you have to choose from a list of options. Delete those not applicable and give details of those which do apply.

Section E asks for details which may affect the tax position and is self-explanatory.

Section F is simply a declaration to be signed by applicants.

The cheque for the IHT due, that is, the extra amount of tax should be returned with the forms, if it is to be paid at once.

The second copy of Cap 30 will later be returned to you with the certificate signed and stamped. You can now feel assured that the capital taxes office will not be claiming further tax at a later date.

Paying off debts

Any outstanding mortgage on a house is a debt of the estate if the will specified that the house was to be bequeathed free of any outstanding mortgage.

Other debts may include funeral expenses and household bills for gas, electricity, telephone, outstanding hire-purchase payments and so on.

These can be paid as sufficient assets come into the estate's account. In the case of hire-purchase payments, you would have a choice of paying off the whole debt or continuing the payments in instalments from the estate in the name(s) of the executor(s).

Redeeming a house mortgage

You may be required by the will to redeem the mortgage on the deceased's house before it passes into the hands of a beneficiary. The will may have specified that the deceased's house for example should pass to a beneficiary free of any liability for any outstanding mortgage. The outstanding mortgage is paid as a debt of the estate.

As executor, you should write to the organization or company who gave the mortgage, explaining that you are executor and wish to redeem the mortgage. You should ask them to inform you of the exact amount that will be outstanding on the date when you expect to write them a cheque to clear the debt. This might be two weeks from the date of your initial letter. The exact amount should include interest due and payments outstanding that had not been paid because the deceased's account had been closed at death.

Once the company or organization have let you know

the amount involved, you will write back stating that you are enclosing the official copy of the grant (and request its return) and the cheque for the appropriate amount.

You will also request that the mortgage is discharged and that all the relevant documents are sent to you.

You should also arrange house insurance. This can be done by transferring any existing policy in the deceased's name to that of the beneficiary. Alternatively, a new policy could be taken out.

Transferring the house

The house may be a registered or an unregistered property. A registered property is one which is registered at the land registry. The deeds will have with them a land certificate. If the property is mortgaged, the institution which gave the mortgage will hold a charge certificate, rather than deeds.

When the mortgage on a house with a registered title is completely paid, the mortgage company, or bank or building society send the owner two documents. The first is the charge certificate. The second is form 53, a land registry form acknowledging payment of the mortgage. Both should be sent to the land registry who will in time send the land certificate confirming ownership.

When someone dies bequeathing their house which is registered in their name, executors must send an official copy of the grant to the land registry, to prove that they act in place of the deceased.

The land registry should be informed if you have redeemed the mortgage. They must also be told that you are executor, and informed of the proposed new owner of the house.

All this is done on Assent or Appropriation HM Land Registry (form 56) obtainable from Oyez Stationery.

The same form is used where the house is leasehold. The landlord must be informed and if the lease so requires, he could demand a copy of the completed form 56 and a fee.

Form 56 requires you to enter the following details:

- title number (the address of the property)
- the value of the property
- the name(s) of the executor(s)
- the name and address of the deceased
- the name and address of the beneficiary

It has to be dated and signed by the executor(s) in the presence of a witness.

You should then write to the land registry stating that you enclose these documents:

1 Official copy of the grant (asking for its return)
2 The charge certificate for the property
3 Form 53 (acknowledging the mortgage is paid up)
4 Form 56
5 The appropriate fee. The cheque is made out to HM Land Registry

You request the land registry to cancel the mortgage and register the named beneficiary as the new owner of the property.

The land registry fee is for arranging the transaction. It is on a sliding scale depending on the value of the house being transferred or bought.

The relevant value fees and land registry fees for 1989 are given below. For current fees, contact your local Citizens Advice Bureau or the land registry.

Value fees and land registry fees (1989)

Value fee (£)	Land registry fee (£)
0 - 80,000	25
80,001 - 90,000	28
90,001 - 100,000	32
100,001- 150,000	36
150,001 - 200,000	40
200,001 - 300,000	45
300,001 - 400,000	50
400,001 - 500,000	55
500,001 - 600,000	60 etc

Under the provisions of the will, the executor or administrator may be left the property. When form 56 is completed the form transfers the property from the deceased to the executor and then from the executor to the new owner.

What happens if the property is unregistered? Let us assume that you have paid off any mortgage outstanding on the deceased's property. Identify the deed which was drafted when the house was purchased by the deceased and which transferred ownership to him or her. In the case of a leasehold property the document is known as an assignment.

Next, identify the mortgage deed which has a receipt at the back of it to confirm that the mortgage has been cleared. You also need the original grant of probate. Now you need to prepare a document called an assent which transfers the ownership of the property to the person entitled to it.

Assent

I (*personal representative's full name*) of (*personal representative's full address*) as personal representative of (*name of deceased*) late of (*deceased's address*) aforesaid deceased who died on the (*date, month and year of death*) and probate of whose will/letters of administration to whose estate with the will annexed was/were granted to me by the District Probate Registry at (*location of registry*) do hereby as personal representative of the deceased assent to the freehold property (*full address of property*) in (*full name of beneficiary*) of (*beneficiary's address*).

I hereby acknowledge (*beneficiary's full name*) right to the production of probate/letters of administration.

Signed by the executor(s) of the will of (*deceased's name*) deceased: (*name(s), address(es), and occupation(s) of executor(s)*)
(*signature of executor(s)*)
(*signature, name and address of witness*)

Should an assent be written for a leashold house, it must include details of the lease. The landlord should be informed. He may be within his rights to require you to give him a copy of the assent and a certain sum. This all depends on exactly what the lease says.

The assent is necessary even where the beneficiary is a personal representative in which case you may have to write an assent to yourself.

If the property is jointly owned by joint-tenants an assent is not normally required. The deceased's death certificate should be filed with the deeds to indicate the passing of the deceased's joint-tenancy.

An assent should not be used if there is an outstanding mortgage or any other likely difficulty.

Nothing further has to be done in connection with the assent except to keep it with the deeds.

Whether the title is registered or not, a note of the assent should be written on the back of the original grant.

It might read as follows:

An assent dated (*insert date*) vested the freehold house (*full address of house*) in (*name of beneficiary*). His/Her right to produce this grant of probate was acknowledged.

This gives the beneficiary the right to see the original grant. If he wishes to sell the house, he would need the grant to show that he owned the property.

It may be best to seek professional advice to prepare an assent for an unregistered house. Should the executors die before the house is sold and the assent is found to be incorrect, this could create real difficulties.

There may be an outstanding mortgage at the date of the deceased's death, and the will may not specify that the mortgage should be paid off from the residue of the estate. Where this is the case, the house may have to be sold to clear the mortgage. The balance left when the proceeds of the sale have been used to pay off the mortgage, would then go to the beneficiary.

Alternatively the beneficiary could take up the payments on the existing mortgage or apply for a new mortgage from either the same source or an alternative one.

If a house is transferred to a beneficiary who then sells it, capital gains tax may become due. The 'gain' is calculated as any increase in value between the probate value and the new selling price.

This can be partly or wholly offset. Costs such as legal fees and estate agents charges can be deducted. There is also a threshold under which executors are not liable for tax.

In 1990, this was £5,000.

The current threshold can be determined from the local citizens advice bureau.

The executor's tax return would show the gross gain, costs and net gain.

Stocks and shares

It may be that the will has specified to whom shares are to be left and how they are to be divided.

But some or all shares may have to be sold to pay off debts, IHT and probate fees, to meet the expenses of administering the estate or to pay legacies. Where this is necessary, it is the remaining shares which are distributed according to the will.

Should it be necessary to sell shares to meet such obligations, you should write to the registrar of the company concerned, enclosing an official copy of the grant. In the case of government stock, the registrar is the Bank of England.

You obtain a stock transfer form for each batch of shares and sign it in order to be able to sell the shares. Stock transfer forms are available from Oyez Stationers (form Con 40). The form can be enclosed when you send the official copy of the grant to the registrar.

Shares should be sold through a broker, either with a

broking firm or through a bank. Check the commission rates and any other fees involved before you finally decide who should deal for you.

A list should be kept of the shares involved, their value at the date of the deceased's death, the price at which they were sold, the cost of commission and other fees and the net loss or gain. This will be useful should capital gains tax become due.

If shares (or unit trusts) are sold at a loss within a year of the deceased's death by executors, a claim can be made against IHT. The total of the gross selling price of the shares sold within the year is noted. This amount may be substituted for the value for IHT. The alteration to IHT is made by a corrective document.

When stocks and shares have to be sold, a fall in market value can be turned to the advantage of the estate. Some 40% of the drop in value can be saved.

Even if stocks and shares are not sold, the relevant company registrar has to be sent a copy of the grant. Where shares are to be transferred directly to beneficiaries specified in the will, the transfer of shares should be sent to the registrar at the same time as the grant.

Formal transfer of shares is not normally necessary when the sole executor is the person given shares by the will. A 'letter of request' is used instead. Oyez Stationery publish these as form Conveyancing 41A. It is a pink, single page, self-explanatory form.

If shares are to be divided equally among beneficiaries as a part of the estate's residue, they should be revalued at the date that administration ends. This is when all debts are paid and all taxes sorted out. The accounts should show this. Perhaps the most equitable way of dividing shares is to subdivide each company shareholding.

Such a division may not always be possible. In certain trusts, to split the holding may be to reduce the subdivided holdings to a lower level than the trust allows.

One way to resolve this problem is to sell the units and divide the cash released equitably between beneficiaries.

A stock transfer form (Conveyancing 40) should be completed for each of the stocks held in order to register the beneficiary as the new owner. If the stock is to be divided among more than one beneficiary, then a separate form must be completed for each beneficiary. These must be sent to each company registrar concerned along with an official copy of the grant.

Each form requires that the company name are entered. Details of the unit trust or government stock are entered instead where appropriate. The number of the holding is entered and the type of security (e.g. ordinary share). The name of the transferors of the security is entered. The executor(s) are the transferors in this case and will be accepted as such where the official copy of the grant is also presented. The name and address of the transferee is entered. The form must be endorsed, choosing from a list of options A to M which are printed on the form.

Example 1

If the stocks and shares are a 'specific devise or legacy':

> I hereby certify that this transaction in respect of which this transfer is made is one which falls within category B above.

This category listed 'above' on the form refers to the Stamp Duty (Exempt Instruments) Regulations 1987.

Example 2

Where the stocks and shares form part of the 'residuary estate of a testator':
As for (1) but substitute category E for category B.

Example 3

Where stocks and shares are transferred under the rules of intestacy:
As for (1) but substitute category C.

The relevant companies will return new stock and share certificates under the names of the new owners.

Stocks and shares (or any asset) may be sold at a higher price than the price at which they were bought or probate value (their value at the date of the deceased's death). If this arises, then capital gains tax becomes payable.

The amount of gain on which tax is payable can be reduced. The original value can be increased in parallel with the increase in the retail price index.

There are several ways in which capital gains tax may be avoided or reduced. Shares may be due for transfer to beneficiaries and may have increased in value. They could be sold within the estate and the cash yielded could then be paid to the beneficiaries who could then buy back the shares at their 'higher' value. This value would then be the one from which any gains would be calculated if the beneficiaries sold at a profit in the future. Dealing fees and commissions should be borne in mind when working out if such a strategy would be advantageous.

Another point can help reduce capital gains tax. For each tax year (6 April to the 5 April of the following year) each person is entitled to a certain threshold of gains before tax becomes payable. Losses can be offset against gains.

In 1988–89 the threshold was £5,000.

The most recent figures can be obtained from the local citizens advice bureau.

Also the executors have a similar threshold before tax is payable which is in the tax year in which the deceased died, and also in each of the two subsequent tax years.

This can be used to advantage if the beneficiaries expect gains in any of these three years. The shares could be held by the estate. They might then be sold at a gain over a three-year period using the executors' exemptions totalling a possible three times the annual threshold over the three years.

---

ie £15,000 on 1988–89 figures.

No capital gains tax is payable on Treasury stock or

exchequer stock or on gilts.

Income tax return form R59

Get form R59 from the Inland Revenue. This is a tax return which will cover the financial year in which the deceased died, from 6 April to 5 April the following year.

If the deceased died say in May, it may be that the administration of the estate is completed within the time span of the one form. If however, the death occurred say in March, it is likely that you will need two forms. One would cover the first period of the administration, in our example about a month. The second form would cover the second period of the administration.

The form is completed to relate to the completion of administration. Distribution of the estate does not have to have already taken place. It is only necessary that debts and liabilities have been ascertained.

The form R59 concerns income tax and capital gains tax. All income on the estate is subject to basic rate income tax.

In 1990 this was 25%.

The Inland Revenue will inform you of the current rate. Interest on any loan secured to pay IHT and probate fees may be deducted from income tax due.

Capital gains tax is due on gains which are chargeable and were realized by the sale of assets in the estate.

In 1990 executors were allowed a £5,000 threshold before CGT became payable.

This allowance applies for the year in which death occurred and the two subsequent years. The inland revenue will inform you of the current threshold.

Income to the estate which has already been taxed at

source, need not be declared on the form. This includes dividend cheques from companies. These will have had a certificate attached to them when they were sent to you indicating that tax had already been paid.

Bank or building society interest is taxed at source also, hence the gross and net figures which are displayed to attract savers.

We will now return to the items on which tax can be reclaimed: interest on the loan for IHT and probate fees. If, for example, £200 was paid in interest, you are entitled to a refund of the basic rate of tax.

The rate in 1990 was 25%. Using this rate, £50 would be due.

This assumes that tax has already been paid on some assets. It is that tax in a sense which you are claiming back.

If dividends have been received from stocks and shares, these will have had tax deducted at the basic rate of income tax. If this exceeds the amount you proposed, you may claim for a refund. Send the counterfoils to the inspector of taxes.

With reference to capital gains tax, make a list of the shares you have sold. Note their value as itemized in form Cap 44. Also note the date of each sale and the proceeds of the sale of each share, once commissions and other costs have been taken off.

If there is a gain from these sales, the amount should be entered on form R59.

Remember the threshold under which you pay no GGT.

In 1990 this was £5,000.

The Inland Revenue will send a cheque for the amount of the refund and will return the evidence of tax credit, that is, the dividend payment counterfoils.

You use these counterfoils in preparing the final cash

distribution to beneficiaries.

You should also forward to beneficiaries the tax deduction certificates for income tax paid in the estate on income received.

Distribution

Before distribution, you should be sure that no one is going to make a claim on the estate under the Inheritance (Provision for Family and Dependants) Act 1975.

Even though the deceased's will may have been fulfilled or the rules of intestacy followed, there may be grounds for a claim if someone considers they have not been reasonably provided for.

Except under very exceptional circumstances, any such claims must be made within six months of probate being granted. The safest approach, if there is the possibility of such a claim, is to delay distribution until six months after probate was granted.

Once all expenses and debts have been paid, you make the distribution according to the will, obtaining receipts for everything that does not involve formal transfer.

Receipts should be obtained for such items as the following:

- administration expenses
- furniture and household effects
- particular bequests

Legacies to minors (under eighteen years old) cannot legally be paid to them but should be invested by executors until the person reaches the age of majority. The money and any interest it has earned can then be transferred from the executors' hands to the person benefiting. Again, a receipt should be obtained.

If circumstances dictate that the legacy cannot be paid for some years a special arrangement comes into force. When the legatee receives the legacy he/she is also entitled to the capital sum plus 6% per annum beginning from the year following the date of the death to the time the legacy is paid.

The legatee has to declare this as taxable income. As executor, you can set this off against any income tax due on income earned in the administration.

Accounts

The accounts of the estate draw together the information needed to demonstrate that administration and distribution have taken place satisfactorily.

It is sensible to have three accounts: a capital account, an income account and a distribution account. Each is divided into a section for receipts and for payments.

In the capital account receipts section is listed all the assets at the date of death, and the value of these is itemized and totalled.

In the payments section the value of payments are itemized and totalled. Payments include the balance to be carried over to the distribution account. If the total receipts for example were £200,000 and the payments were £50,000, the total of payments would be made up to £200,000 to balance with receipts, by adding the item 'paid to distribution account' £150,000.

The income account receipts section lists all items on which there was an income after the deceased's death, and before distribution. Some of these items attract tax so should be listed as in the example below.

Item	Gross	Tax credit	Net
	£	£	£
Dividends on stocks and shares received after death	400	100	300

The tax credits can then be totalled separately from the net receipts. When an item is taxed at source, simply enter its value in the net column. The tax credit due to each beneficiary can then be worked out more easily. This is done by totalling the tax credits then deducting the tax repayment on the executor's loan. This gives the tax credit for deduction certificate form R185 E. The payments in the income account section are listed in the normal way and totalled. These might include interest on the executor's loan and interest to close a mortgage account. Any excess of receipts over payments is transferred to the capital account and listed under its receipts. This amount should be entered in the income account payment section so that the total receipts and the total payments in the income account are identical.

The distribution account will show the receipts are the total value of the estate to be distributed.

Payments will list the items to be given out and their value. Their total should of course match that of the receipts.

You and any other executors sign the accounts and send a copy to each residual beneficiary along with their appropriate cheque.

Ask for a receipt. Once the cheques are cleared, the executors account will be empty and you can close it.

All the relevant papers, probate and signed accounts should be kept for twelve years.

There may be life interests under a trust in the will. If so, note the date of the final distribution at the death of anyone with a life interest. Then keep the papers for a further twelve years.

Form R185E

Form R185E comprises income tax deduction certificates.

The beneficiaries entitled to the residuary estate are also entitled to, as part of this residuary, any income earned by the estate.

You have paid basic rate income tax

25% in 1990.

on all the income with the exception of the interest on the bank loan taken out to pay IHT and probate fees.

You know the total tax credit in the estate for deduction certificate R185E. This is divided among residual beneficiaries.

The form is completed as follows. Under 'trust' enter 'the estate of the deceased (*name of deceased*)'. For 'income', state 'gross income from which tax has been deducted' and write in the amount.

In the next column enter the tax deducted. Net income is entered in the third column.

These figures are calculated using the rate for tax credit.

> *Using 1990 figures, the amount of tax credit would be 25% of the gross income paid from the deceased's estate to the beneficiary. The remainder, once 25% has been deducted from gross income, is the net income (75%).*

You then sign the forms and send them to the beneficiaries.

Obtaining current figures

Current figures are obtained from the local citizens advice bureau

	Previous figures	Current figures
The threshold of capital gains per tax year for each person	£5,000 (in 1988–9)	
Basic rate of income tax	25% (in 1990)	

Distributing the residuary of the estate to beneficiaries

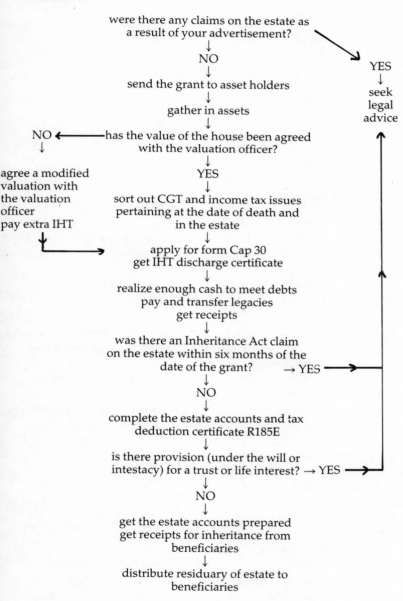

were there any claims on the estate as
a result of your advertisement?

NO → YES → seek legal advice

send the grant to asset holders

gather in assets

NO ← has the value of the house been agreed with the valuation officer?

agree a modified valuation with the valuation officer pay extra IHT

YES

sort out CGT and income tax issues pertaining at the date of death and in the estate

apply for form Cap 30 get IHT discharge certificate

realize enough cash to meet debts pay and transfer legacies get receipts

was there an Inheritance Act claim on the estate within six months of the date of the grant? → YES →

NO

complete the estate accounts and tax deduction certificate R185E

is there provision (under the will or intestacy) for a trust or life interest? → YES →

NO

get the estate accounts prepared get receipts for inheritance from beneficiaries

distribute residuary of estate to beneficiaries

15   Estates in Scotland

Although there are many differences between law and procedures in England and Wales on the one hand and in Scotland on the other, there are some areas where procedure is the same.

These include the seven-year rule which affects gifts given in the deceased's lifetime. Tax issues including the rules for paying IHT and exemption from it are the same. But the differences that still exist are considerable.

The will and its provisions

A boy aged fourteen years or above or a girl aged twelve years or above whose permanent home is in Scotland are able to make a valid will.

A matter known as 'legal rights' can affect the will. It ensures that a person cannot completely disinherit their spouse or descendants. Irrespective of the wishes expressed in the will, a spouse is entitled to a third of the moveable estate. This excludes buildings and land but would include such items as money, jewellery, furniture, paintings and so on. If there are no descendants, then the spouse is entitled to half of the moveable estate. In the same way the children of the deceased have a right to a third of the moveable estate which is shared between them. If the deceased leaves no surviving spouse, then the children's entitlement increases to a third.

It is sometimes more beneficial for the spouse or children to accept the wishes of the will and not apply for legal rights. The bulk of the estate may be in land and property while only a small proportion is 'immoveable'. If the deceased has willed the land and property to the spouse (and children) it may not be financially profitable for them to claim legal rights. They would have to choose between legal rights and the provision specified in the will. It is not permissible to have both. Legal rights are claimed simply by informing the executors.

If the deceased dies intestate and the estate is small, the spouse is entitled to the house, furniture and money left. In such a case, the children have no 'legal right' to a claim on the estate. On the other hand, if exactly the same property had been left to the spouse by a will, the children would be able to claim a third of the moveable estate under their legal rights.

The deceased may have left a bequest to a descendant who at a later date dies before the deceased. The descendant may be the deceased's child or grandchild for example. The bequest would then go automatically to the children of the original beneficiaries. To avoid this, the will would have to make it clear that this was not the deceased's wish.

If the deceased willed a bequest to a nephew and/or niece, the same rule applies.

The matter of co-ownership of property can affect the wishes expressed in a will and may override them.

In Scotland, property owned by two people is owned in common, each owner having a share. When the deceased dies, his or her share passes to the survivor either under the will or under the rules of intestacy. (Joint-holdings involve owners with a common bond such as trustees.)

There is an equivalent to English joint-tenancy. This is common-ownership in which the title to the property specifies that the share belonging to the deceased (whoever is the first to die) should go to the survivor. If this arrangement has been revoked for any reason, for instance the deceased may have bought out the other owner's share, it would be stated in the title.

Unless this is done, the deceased would not normally be able to leave his or her share of the property to anybody except the other common-owner.

The will may be in the testator's handwriting in which

case it would be valid even if only signed by the testator. There need not be the usual two witnesses.

The handwritten will is known as a holograph will. The testator may have typed out the will but made a note above his signature that the will is 'adopted as holograph'. Such a will again needs only the testator's signature.

The same applies to 'holograph' or 'adopted as holograph' codicils to a will.

If someone challenges the authenticity of such a will or codicil, however, proof has to be given of its genuineness.

In the case of a will witnessed by two people, the boot is on the other foot. If anyone challenges it, they have the burden of proof and must be able to demonstrate its lack of authenticity.

The witnesses each have to see the testator sign or hear him acknowledge the signature to be his or her own. Witnesses need not be present together so the testing clause at the end of the will would not specify this.

A beneficiary of the will may also be a witness but this may cause difficulties and could lead to the will being challenged.

Each page of the will should be signed by the testator and the final page signed by the testator and witness (unless it is a holograph or adopted as holograph will).

If the deceased had married after making the will, the will is not automatically revoked by the marriage.

Unless stepchildren are specifically included in a will, they do not benefit, even from 'legal rights'.

Neither are bequests to a spouse automatically cancelled by a subsequent divorce.

The will may have been made by the deceased before one of his/her children was born and it may not indicate that the estate, or part of it, should go to that child. The child may then apply for the will to be set aside which would lead to the estate being divided under intestacy rules. Alternatively, of course, the child may claim legal rights.

On the other hand the will may specifically exclude any children born after the will was made.

There is no public trustee service in Scotland. If you are nominated as executor in a will you will be obliged to carry out this duty unless you decline.

Trustees may not use capital from the estate when the estate is intended for the benefit of the children. Nor may they use it to buy a house unless it is for the children to reside in. The trustees' power to use income is also circumscribed. These restrictions do not apply of course if the will specifically empowers you to use income or/and capital.

In England and Wales, personal representatives nominated in the will to handle the deceased's property are called executors. In Scotland the equivalent term is executors-nominate.

When the deceased dies intestate, the personal representative in England and Wales is known as the administrator. Executor-dative is the term used in Scotland.

Where there is no will, a family member usually has a solicitor to assist in petitioning the court to appoint him (the family member) as executor-dative. This would not be necessary where the estate was small.

> *In 1990 this meant having a gross value of £13,000 or less.*

The gross value is the value before debts are deducted.

Both types of executor have to have their authority confirmed by the sheriff before they can properly act. Before this confirmation, you should take care of the estate and not interfere with the deceased's property or give anything to beneficiaries. Otherwise you could be held personally liable for the deceased's debts.

The liability for debts is limited to the value of the estate when the following are involved:

(a) confirmed executors
(b) executors confirmed later who before confirmation acted within their legal authority and behaved prudently.

The claims on a joint bank account held by the deceased merit particular mention. A claim to ownership hinges on who paid the money into the account and with what intention. Only one of the joint account holders may have paid money into the account enabling the other to sign cheques. The money is then the property of the first holder.

Alternatively, the holders may have intended to pool resources, irrespective of the fact that only one of them put money into the account and the money is then the property of each, equally shared. Such an intention to pool the money, however, has to be proved.

If each account holder contributed and there was no intention to pool, the balance is divided in proportion to the contributions. Where it is too hard to track down who contributed what, the balance is shared equally. If the intention was to pool the money, the balance is equally shared also.

The housekeeping account of a married couple is assumed to be pooled and is shared equally unless other arrangements were specifically made.

Form A3 or B4 and confirmation

The form to apply for confirmation can be obtained from any of the following places: Capital Taxes Office, HM Commissary Office, main post offices and sheriff courts.

Should there be more than one executor, one, in agreement with the other(s) applies for confirmation.

An executor-nominate not wishing to act can decline by sending a signed statement when the forms for confirmation are sent for.

The remaining executor(s) appointed by the will are then confirmed. You cannot decline and at the same time reserve the right to apply at a later date.

If there is only one executor-nominate who does not wish to act he should first get a co-executor and then decline. The remaining executor will then act alone. This saves the cost of applying to the court for another executor to be appointed.

You send for either form A3 or B4.

If the following points apply, the correct form to use is A3:

(a)   The estate is not a 'small' one
(b)   The estate does not come within the remit of form B4

If the following criteria apply, you should apply for form B4:

(a)   The value of the estate is no higher than the specified amount

> *In 1990 the amount was £70,000.*

(b)   The deceased.had no interest in settled property
(c)   The deceased made no chargeable lifetime transfers
(d)   The deceased had no property outside the United Kingdom valued at more than a certain amount

> *In 1990 the relevant value was £10,000.*

Form A3

Cap form A3 has twelve pages. Page 1 simply asks for information about the deceased and executors. Page 2 consists of statements which you have to swear to. The page is then signed by the 'deponent' and the person administering the oath.

Pages 3 and 4 ask for information about the deceased's property and other matters. There are eight sections as follows:

1 Gifts
2 Gifts with reservation
3 Settled property
4 Joint property
5 Nominations
6 Deduction of liabilities
7 Surviving relatives

8 Deceased domiciled in Scotland

Pages 5, 6 and 7 are for an inventory in which property must be listed in the following order:

Heritable estate in Scotland (i.e. land and buildings)
Moveable estate in Scotland (e.g. cash, furniture, government stock, etc.)
Real estate in England and Wales (i.e. land and buildings)
Personal estate in England and Wales
Real estate in Northern Ireland
Personal estate in Northern Ireland
Summary for confirmation
Estate elsewhere (stating in which country)

As well as listing each item you must include its value.

Pages 8 and 9 together consist of three sections:
1 The net estate in the United Kingdom.
2 The net estate outside the United Kingdom.
3 Any other property on which tax is payable (or would be payable) if the estate is over the tax threshold and is not included in the inventory. Subsections on settled property, gifts with reservation, lifetime chargeable transfers and 'other property'.
  At the bottom of page 9 is a declaration to be signed by the 'deponing executor'.

Pages 10, 11 and 12 consist of six sections A to F:
A 'Summary of chargeable transfers'. These are carried forward from section 1, 2 and 3 on pages 8 and 9.
B Net tax due on death estate.
C Death estate on which tax is to be paid on this form.
D The instalment option.
E The total tax and interest to be paid on non-instalment-option property and instalment-option property, including chargeable transfers within seven years of death.
F Summary of amounts to be paid on the form.

Form B4

Cap form B4 consists of eight pages. Page 1 and 2 are exactly the same as for Form A3.

Page 3 comprises four subsections:

1 Joint property
2 Nominations
3 Deduction of liabilities
4 Surviving relations

Page 4 and 5 ask for an inventory set out in the same way as for form A3.

Pages 6 and 7 are made up of three sections:

1 The net estate in the United Kingdom.
2 The net estate outside the UK.
3 All other property. The foot of page 7 comprises a section covering a 'summary of chargeable transfers'. There is a declaration to be signed by the deponing executor.

The final page of the form gives guidance on what are Excepted Estates.

After completing form A3 or B4

Regarding IHT, there should be none to pay on estates where you needed to complete form B4.

Tax on A3 estates needs to be paid before you can apply for confirmation. The A3 form and a cheque made in favour of the inland revenue should be sent to the Capital Taxes Office.

Subsequently, the Capital Taxes Office will return the form which will have been stamped to show that you have paid the tax. Any adjustments that may need to be made to the amount of tax paid can be arranged later.

Once the appropriate form A3 or B4 is completed and

any IHT due is paid, you have to take the form (and the will) to someone qualified to administer oaths. If the will is a holograph will you also need sworn statements by two people to state its authenticity.

The oath may be sworn before the following:

(a) notaries public
(b) solicitors who are notaries public
(c) justices of the peace
(d) officials in the sheriff court qualified to take executors' oaths
(e) judges

The purpose of the oath is to confirm that the information you have set down in the form is complete and accurate, and that you know of no other wills and codicils except those mentioned on the form.

Both you and the person administering the oath sign the form and other documents. Page 2 of the form is then completed which concerns the taking of the oath.

Next, identify the sheriff court which is local to the place where the deceased was domiciled when he/she died. Send or personally take the following to the clerk of that court:

(a) The form A3 or B4
(b) The will
(c) The two statements if the will is a holograph

You must pay for confirmation. Fees are shown below.

Fees for Confirmation
Scotland

Value of Estate	Fee
£13,000–£20,000	£20
over £20,000	£50 + £20 for each £10,000 or part of £10,000 over £20,000

A week or two later, if all runs smoothly the

confirmation and the will should be posted to you, either together or separately.

Certificates of confirmation can be ordered for separate items of the estate if they are numerous. Information as to the cost of these can be obtained from the Capital Taxes Office.

Once you have the certificate(s) send it/them to all the holders of the deceased's assets, so they can release the assets to you.

When confirmation is unnecessary

Confirmation is not needed in the circumstances outlined below:

1 Payments of up to a certain amount by such bodies as the Department for National Savings, according to the same rules as those applying to England and Wales.

In 1990 the threshold amount was £5,000.

---

2 Property held in common by the deceased and another person on a title which has a survivorship destination. The property goes directly to the surviving owner, but the share is disclosed for tax purposes.

However, confirmation is required for the deceased's share of property held in common with another person, where there is no survivorship destination.

Even if confirmation is needed for only one item, a full inventory must be made of all the deceased's cash and personal effects.

If the deceased dies intestate

Should there be no will, a relative of the deceased is appointed as executor by the court.

A surviving spouse inheriting the whole estate by prior rights can insist on being sole executor. Prior rights are rights to the deceased's property when there is no will.

If other family members share in the estate, the surviving spouse is still usually an executor. Additional executors can also be appointed.

What if there is no surviving spouse? Then the children can be appointed.

The surviving spouse may be unable to take on the role of executor. If so, the stipulations for allowing an adult child to become executor may differ from one court to the next. One court may want evidence that the surviving spouse is indeed incapacitated. Another may insist on the surviving spouse giving up his or her rights to the estate if the children are not entitled to a share.

If neither the surviving spouse, nor children are appointed, a relative inheriting all or part of the estate assumes the responsibility.

The relative petitions the sheriff court responsible for the area in which the deceased was domiciled. A solicitor will prepare the petition for a fee, and the court will grant the petition within a week if all goes smoothly.

An executor appointed by the court must give a 'bond of caution' (a guarantee) that they will carry out executor's duties correctly. Only then will confirmation be issued.

The cautioner may be an insurance company who will act for a premium related to the value of the estate. They usually prefer that a solicitor applies for caution on the executor's behalf.

Should you be executor in such circumstances the cautioner would cover any losses caused through your negligence (or even fraud). They would then try to recoup their losses from you.

A surviving spouse inheriting the whole estate by prior rights need not get a bond of caution.

Small estates

For small estates a simpler procedure is followed.

If the deceased did not make a larger number of

chargeable lifetime gifts, no IHT will be due. (If the deceased died intestate, you need not petition the court to be appointed executor.)

The staff of any sheriff's court will fill in the forms for you. It may not be convenient for you to attend in person. If so, you can apply by post. The sheriff court for the place where the deceased was domiciled is the proper place to apply.

1 You provide the sheriff court with a list of items in the estate and their value, a list of debts, the deceased's name and address, date of birth, date and place of death and the will.
2 The sheriff clerk fills in form B3. You either sign it immediately or he may ask you to return a day or two later.
3 You pay a fee if the estate is above a certain amount. No fee is payable for estates below that value.

> *In 1990 the threshold amount was £3,000 and the fee was £20.*

4 A day or two after you have signed the form, the will and confirmation will be posted to you.

Should there be no will the court appoints an executor. If you are to be executor there is no need to petition the court.

The steps are then as follows:

1 The same as 1 previously.
2 The sheriff clerk completes form B3 for you and asks you to come back a few days later with two witnesses. They must swear to your identity and your relationship with the deceased.
3 The same as step 3 previously.
4 You lodge a bond of caution unless you are the surviving spouse inheriting the whole estate through prior rights.

5 The confirmation is then posted to you.

Debts

The debts of the estate must be paid in an order of priority.

Secured debts such as a mortgage loan secured on property must be paid first. If these are not met the creditor can sell the asset to recoup his loss.

Privileged debts are next in priority. These include the following:

1 medical and funeral expenses
2 the cost of confirmation
3 value added tax debts owed to the government
4 if the deceased was an employer, the wages owed to any employee (up to a certain amount for each employee)

Privileged debts can be paid as soon as sufficient money is released to the estate.

Next ordinary debts should be dealt with. Strictly speaking you do not have to pay ordinary debts until six months after the deceased has died. All creditors are then entitled to equal treatment. If there were insufficient funds to meet all the ordinary debts, this avoids paying on an inequitable first-come first-served basis.

The legal rights of certain relatives constitute possible debts.

Those entitled to claim legal rights are the surviving spouse, children (including adopted ones and those born outside marriage) and other descendants.

Draw up a list of everyone who could claim. Write to them and inform them how much the legal rights are worth. You should also advise them to take legal advice on the question of whether they should renounce or claim the rights.

A young person under the age of eighteen has to obtain the consent of parents to make the 'renounce or claim' decision. A boy younger than 14 and a girl below 12 cannot legally make the decision. Where the legal rights involve large sums of money, you can invest a sum of money equal to that which could be claimed under legal rights. When the young person reaches the age of eighteen, they can then decide whether to renounce or to claim.

Where less substantial sums are involved, but where the legal rights exceed a certain sum, say around £2,000, the amount can be put into the care of the surviving spouse in their capacity as guardian to the child.

If there are possible creditors unknown to you, an advertisement could be placed in local newspapers.

Once six months has elapsed since the death, you can pay creditors and distribute the rest of the estate to beneficiaries.

If creditors claim after the six months, they are entitled to be paid if there is still estate in your hands.

Should no estate be left, clearly late creditors cannot be paid. Only if it can be shown that you should have known about the existence of the late creditor would he have a claim. If such a claim were successful, the money would be claimed against you as executor.

The transfer of the house

If the house of the deceased was co-owned and the title had a survivorship destination, then the deceased's share goes automatically to the surviving co-owner.

The house may be transferred in two other main ways:

1 It is transferred to a person who benefits under the deceased's will or under intestacy rules, or who is claiming it under legal rights.
2 It is transferred to a person who does not fall into any of the categories in 1, for instance someone wishing to buy the house.

In the second case, a solicitor should be asked to prepare a document known as a disposition.

In the first case, you can transfer the house using a

document called a docket. This is a form written (or typed) on the back of the certificate of confirmation concerning the house. Failing this the back of the confirmation may be used.

Irrespective of whether the house title is registered in the land register for Scotland or the sasine register, the docket takes the same form.

Essentially the docket sets out one of four possible entitlements of the transferee (the person to whom part or all of the property is being transferred).

These are that the transfer is made to satisfy one of the following:

1 in (part) satisfaction of his/her claim to prior rights, as a surviving spouse on the death of the deceased.
2 in (part) satisfaction of his/her claim to legal rights on the death of the deceased.
3 in (part) satisfaction of his/her share of the estate
4 in (part) implementation of the will of the deceased dated (*insert the date of the will*)

Once the appropriate type of entitlement has been decided from 1 2 3 or 4 above, the docket is completed as follows:

Docket

I (*executor's full name*) being by virtue of the within certificate of confirmation the executor of the estate of (*deceased's full name*) so far as specified in the confirmation hereby nominate (*transferee's full name and address*) as the person entitled (*insert the appropriate entitlement from choices 1, 2, 3, or 4*) to the following item of estate, that is to say (*postal address of the house*) being number (*item number of the house in the inventory of the estate*) of the items of estate specified in the said confirmation.

In witness hereof I have signed this docket at (*place of signing*) on (*date of signing*) before the following witnesses

(*first witness's full name and address*) and (*second witness's full
name and address*).

First witness's signature

Executory's signature

Second witness's signature

You sign the docket first in the presence of the two
witnesses who then sign it themselves.

The docket can then be given to the transferee. If you
are the transferee, the docket transfers the house from
you, in your role as executor, to you as an individual.

The house may be registered in the land register for
Scotland or it may be unregistered. If it is registered, the
transferee applies to have it put in his or her name by
sending the docket and the certificate of confirmation to
the Keeper (address at end of book).

To discharge a building society loan on a registered
house, the procedure is similar to that for England and
Wales.

Should the land be unregistered, the transferee can
show the docket as evidence of their ownership, if and
when they sell the house.

To discharge a building society loan on unregistered
land, the building society sends you a 'discharge'. This
document should be recorded in the sasine register.

Whether the property is registered or not, the docket
can be registered for safe keeping in the Books of Council
and Session. This is a national register of deeds. Send the
docket to the Registers of Scotland who will keep the
docket and send you back a copy.

Legacies

If an executor has unreasonably delayed paying a legacy,
the legatee can claim interest on the legacy, at a rate
calculated according to the average earnings of the estate.

A legacy for a boy under 14 or a girl under 12 can be paid

to the parents to invest for the child. A young person older than this but under the age of eighteen can receive the legacy directly. But the young person and the parent should sign to confirm that the legacy was received.

If the will allows the executor to pay a child's legacy to the parents, this can be done.

Documents of transfer of shares should be sent to the Controller of Stamps (Scotland).

Distribution of intestacy

If there is no will, the executor(s)–nominate distribute the deceased's estate according to the intestacy rules laid out in the Succession (Scotland) Act 1964.

A few general points need to be remembered before we look at details.

A 'relative' includes a person linked to the deceased by births outside marriage as well as someone linked by births within marriage. A divorced person does not inherit from their ex-spouse under intestacy rules.

Also, consider the case of a husband judicially separated from his wife. He is not entitled to inherit any of her intestate property which she acquired after the separation. On the other hand there is no such rule preventing a judicially separated wife inheriting.

If the deceased leaves no spouse

Should the deceased have no surviving spouse, the estate goes to surviving relatives in an order of priority as the list below indicates.

1 Children

Children are defined for this purpose to include adopted children but to exclude step-children.

The deceased's children inherit the estate in equal shares.

If a child died before the deceased, that child's children will inherit the share.

Should all the children be dead, then the grandchildren inherit equal shares. The children of a deceased grandchild inherit the share that would have gone to their dead parent.

2 Brothers, sisters and parents

If both of the deceased's parents are dead, the deceased's estate is shared among his brothers and sisters.

The children of a dead brother or sister inherit their dead parents' share.

If there are no full brothers or sisters, then any half-brothers or sisters can inherit.

A child jointly adopted by a couple is considered the full brother or sister of any of their other children.

No brothers and sisters or nieces and nephews may survive. In this case the deceased's parents inherit the estate in equal shares. Should only one parent survive in these circumstnaces he or she inherits the whole estate.

If there are surviving brothers and sisters and surviving parents the estate is split in two. Each half is then divided as explained above.

3 Uncles and aunts

Uncles and aunts of the deceased are next in the chain of inheritance.

If an uncle or aunt died before the deceased then their children (the deceased's cousins) inherit what would have been their parent's share. It is divided equally among them.

If the deceased's cousins are dead, then their children inherit what would have been their parent's share.

4 Grandparents

The deceased's grandparents are next, sharing the estate equally between them. If only one survives then he or she inherits the whole estate.

5 Distant Relatives

Great uncles and great aunts come next. If they are dead, then their children inherit what would have been their parent's share.

If those children are dead then their children in turn inherit in their place.

6 The Crown

If no surviving relatives are traced, the estate goes to the Queen's and Lord Treasurer's Remembrancer, who advertises for claimants. If there is no response, the Crown can award property from the estate to those without a legal claim but who may have a moral claim. The Inheritance (Provision for Family and Dependants) Act 1975 does not apply in Scotland.

If the deceased leaves a spouse

The estate of a deceased person dying intestate and leaving a surviving spouse is distributed in the following priority order.

1 Prior rights

The surviving spouse's prior rights are to the house, its furnishings and a cash sum.

The deceased may have owned the house or a share of it. The surviving spouse is entitled to that house or share providing the following conditions apply:
(a)   the property is in Scotland
(b)   the surviving spouse was ordinarily resident in the property at the date of the deceased's death
(c)   the house (or share of it) is worth less than a certain amount.

In 1990 this was £65,000.

What if the value is more than this? The surviving spouse then gets the maximum amount

---

i.e. £65,000 in 1990.

---

instead of the whole property (or a share of it).

The house may be part of a larger property run as a business where it would be detrimental to separate off the house. If so, the surviving spouse gets the value of the house up to the maximum amount instead of the house itself.

The house may be security for a loan. In this case, the surviving spouse gets the value of the house minus the balance remaining on the loan. The deceased may have had a life policy to clear the loan at death, but this does not affect the matter. The surviving spouse still gets only the net value of the house.

Furnishings do not include cars or jewellery. The surviving spouse gets up to a specified amount of furnishings owned by the deceased, irrespective of whether these were in a house owned by the deceased.

> *In 1990 this amount was £12,000.*

Should the value of furnishings exceed the relevant amount, the surviving spouse can choose items up to the appropriate limit.

A widow or widower is entitled, under prior rights, to a specified amount of cash if the deceased left children or other descendants.

> *In 1990 this sum was £21,000.*

Otherwise the surviving spouse is entitled to a larger cash sum.

> *In 1990 this was £35,000.*

Legal rights

After prior rights have been taken, legal rights come into force.

The surviving spouse is entitled to half of the net moveable estate, if there are no surviving children or other descendants of the deceased. Otherwise the spouse gets one third and the children share a third between them, usually equal shares.

Should one of the deceased's children die before the deceased, leaving children of their own, the share would go to them.

If all the deceased's children have died, the grandchildren get equal shares.

A child renouncing his or her legal rights while the deceased was alive, forfeits his or her share and that of his or her descendants. The deceased may have given a child a sizeable lifetime gift and this too can affect that child's share in legal rights.

What is the net moveable estate? It is estate property excepting land and buildings, and its value has to be worked out before shares can be made. The other kind of estate, you will recall is heritable estate, that is, land and property.

Difficulties arise because the various debts and liabilities of the estate have to be offset against either the heritable or the moveable estate, depending on the particular debt or liability. Some debts and liabilities are set against both heritable and moveable estate.

For example, the heritable estate meets the debt of a loan given against property as security. Moveable estate meets funeral expenses.

IHT and administration costs are covered by both kinds of estate. The relative proportion from each estate is related to their respective value as a proportion of the whole estate.

The deceased may have owned heritable estate other than the house. A sum may have been allocated under prior rights. If so, it is considered to have been taken from both heritable and moveable estate.

> *The sums allocated under prior rights in 1990 were either £21,000 or £35,000 as explained earlier.*

The rest of the estate

If there is any estate left after prior rights, and legal rights have been met, it goes to the nearest relatives of the deceased.

These are in order of priority: children, grandchildren, remoter descendants, brother and sisters of their descendants, and parents.

The allocation made to these relatives is the same as if the deceased had left no spouse.

Should there be no surviving relatives in the order explained above, then the estate goes to the surviving spouse.

Current figures

The current figure for item 5 below is obtainable from the sheriff court. Figures for all remaining items can be obtained from the capital taxes office in Edinburgh.

	Circumstances	1990 figures	Current figures
		Gross value of	
1	A small estate	£13,000 or less	
2	Value for a B4 estate	£70,000 or less	
3	Value of property out-side United Kingdom for a B4 estate	£10,000 or less	
4	Value for which con-firmation may not be necessary	£5,000 or less	
5	Fee payable to sheriff court if a small estate is valued at more than £3,000	£20	

6	The surviving spouse is entitled to prior rights on the house owned or part-owned by the deceased. The property must be worth less than a threshold amount. (If it is worth more, the surviving spouse gets the threshold amount instead)	£65,000
7	The prior rights of the surviving spouse include a specified amount of furnishings owned by the deceased	£12,000
8	Under prior rights the surviving spouse is entitled to a certain amount of cash if the deceased left descendants	£21,000
9	Under prior rights the surviving spouse is entitled to a certain amount of cash if the deceased left no descendants	£35,000

A footnote

I do hope that you found this book helpful. You may wish to suggest something that would make it more useful to those trying to cope with the death of someone close to them. Alternatively, you may like to share some of your own experiences, which might be included anonymously in any future edition, to reinforce what has been said. If so, please write to me care of my publisher.

Glossary

Administrator

A personal representative of the deceased who was not nominated in a will, but who will handle the deceased's property.

Autopsy

See post-mortem examination.

Beneficiary

Someone who inherits property through a will or under the rules of intestacy. Also someone who will receive property under a trust at some later date.

Bequest

A legacy of houses and/or land.

Bond of caution

In Scotland, if an executor accidentally fails to carry out part of his duties, compensation for any loss incurred is guaranteed by a bond of caution.

Chargeable gift

Property given or bequeathed to another person on which tax may fall due at a later date or at death.

Confirmation

In Scotland, the court gives a personal representative the authority (confirmation) to be executor of the deceased's estate.

Devise

A devise is a legacy of realty.

Distribution

Giving an estate's property to those entitled to receive it. The personal representative distributes to beneficiaries named in a will, or to beneficiaries under intestacy rules if there is no will.

Docket

In Scotland, a note added to a deed.

Estate

The deceased's property.

Execute

To execute a will is to validate it by signing and witnessing it.

Executor

A person nominated in a will to handle the property of that person when the drawer of the will has died.

Heritable property

In Scotland, property comprising land and buildings.

Informant

A person 'qualified' to register a death.

Interest

The right to property. If the interest is unconditional it is known as absolute interest.

Intestate

To die intestate means dying without having made a will.

Issue

A direct descendant.

Joint tenant

A special arrangement for two or more people to be co-owners of property. When one co-owner dies, the entire property goes automatically to the survivor(s). Joint-tenant rights override what may be stated in the will or what intestacy rules dictate.

Laying Out

When the deceased is laid out, the body is washed and its orifices are blocked with cotton wool and a napkin. It is dressed in fresh clothes. Arms and feet are put straight. The hair is brushed and combed, and a man may also be shaved. The eyes are closed and the jaw is supported.

Legacy

Property which is left to others by a will.

Legal rights

In Scotland, these are the rights of certain relatives to a share of the deceased's estate, irrespective of what is said in a will. The line of entitlement begins with the surviving spouse and/or children.

Life interest

Where property is held by a life tenant, the rights to that property are a life interest.

Life tenant

Someone who may use, and benefit from, property during their lifetime. Once the life-tenant dies, another person becomes a life-tenant of the property or its absolute owner. The term property is used in a broad sense and can include interest on investments.

Moveable property

In Scotland, all property except land and buildings.

Pecuniary

Relating to money.

Personal representative

Someone who manages the deceased's estate. An executor is a personal representative appointed by a will. If not so appointed, the personal representative is called an administrator.

Post-mortem examination

Also called an autopsy or a necropsy. An opening is made across the scalp so that the deceased's brain can be examined. The opening is covered over afterwards by the hair. Another opening is made at the front of the body from neck to groin so that the organs of the chest and abdomen can be examined. You can usually view the body afterwards perhaps in a chapel of rest.

Because of the nature of the operation, there may be some changes in the facial appearance of the deceased. The funeral director should advise you of this before you view the body.

Prior rights

In Scotland, if a husband or wife dies intestate, the surviving spouse is entitled to certain items of the deceased's property. This entitlement is known as prior rights.

Procurator fiscal

A low officer in Scotland with duties similar to those of an English coroner.

Real property (realty)

Land, particularly freehold land, along with buildings which may be on it.

Residue

When an estate's legacies and bequests have been handed over to their recipients and all debts and taxes have been paid, anything left over is called the residue.

Small estate

An estate in Scotland, the gross value of which is below a specified amount.

Still birth

A stillborn child is one born after the 28th week of pregnancy who showed no signs of independent life.

Testator

Someone leaving a will.

Trust

Administering a trust involves the trustee(s) having special ownership of property for a time. They will at a later date hand over the property to the ultimate owner(s). While the property is in their charge, the trustee(s) must administer it for the benefit of the eventual beneficiaries.

Further Reading

Chatterton, David A., *Executorship* (Longman, 1989)

Kimner, J., Scriven, G. and Stanfield, R., *Vickery's Law and Accounts of Executors, Administrators and Trustees* (Cassell, 1987)

Parry and Clark, *The Law of Succession* (Sweet and Maxwell, 1988)

Rudinger, Edith (ed.), *What to do When Someone Dies* (Consumers' Association and Hodder and Stoughton, 1989)

Rudinger, Edith (ed.), *Wills and Probate* (Consumers' Association and Hodder and Stoughton, 1988)

Simpson, M., *The Facts of Death* (Prentice Hall, New Jersey, 1979)

Useful Leaflets, Certificates and Forms

Leaflets from the Department of Social Services (DSS)

The following leaflets are free and most are available from the Social Security Office locally. Some can be obtained from the post office. Alternatively the leaflets can be obtained from the Department of Social Services Leaflets Unit.

Bringing up children?   FB 27
Family Credit   FC 1
Guardian's Allowance   NI 14
A Guide to Retirement Pensions   NP 46
Help with NHS Costs   AB 11
Help when Someone Dies   FB 29
Help with the Community Charge   CCR 1
Housing Benefit – Help with Rent and Rates   RR 1
Income Support – Cash Help   SB 1
Invalidity Benefit   NI 16A
National Insurance for Widows   NI 51
NHS Dental Treatment   D 11
NHS Hospital Travel Costs   H 11
NHS Prescriptions   P 11
NHS Sight Tests and Vouchers for Glasses   G 11
NHS Wigs and Fabric Supports   WF 11
One-Parent Benefit   CH 11
Pneumoconiosis, Byssinosis and Some Other Diseases   PN 1
Rates of War Pensions and Allowances   MPL 154
Retiring? Your Pension and Other Benefits   FB 6
Social Security Benefit Rates   NI 196
War Widows and Other Dependants   MPL 152
What to do after a Death   D 49
Which Benefit?   FB 2
Widow's Benefits   NP 45
For Widows and Other Relatives – Industrial Death Benefit   NI 10
Your Benefits as a Widow for the First 26 Weeks   NP 35
Your Benefit as a Widow after the First 26 Weeks   NP 36
Your Retirement Pension if you are Widowed or Divorced   NP 36
Babies and Benefits   FB 8
Maternity Benefits   NI 17A
Sickness Benefit   NI 16
A Guide to Income Support   SB 20

Leaflets from the inland revenue

The following leaflets are obtainable from the local inland revenue office:

Income Tax and One-Parent Families IR 29
Income Tax and Widows IR 23
Income Tax and Capital Gains Tax –
What Happens When Someone Dies IR 45

Other leaflets

Funerals FAIR JOO 45RP
Obtainable from the Office of Fair Trading.
The Work of the Coroner (HMSO) JO151AR
Obtainable from the Home Office.
How to Obtain Probate (HMSO)
Obtainable from probate offices.
Amber Lloyd (1982) *Easing Grief for Oneself and for Other People*
(Obtainable from Cruse)
Margaret Torrie (1979) *Living Through Loss*
(obtainable from Cruse)
The Loss of Your Baby at Birth or Shortly After
SPL 50M 10/85 M20
(obtainable from the Health Education Authority)

Certificates and forms relating to funeral arrangements

Obtainable from the doctor

Medical certificate of the cause of death (if death is not referred to a coroner)
Notice to informant (about who must register death and what information they should give)
Form 35 (stating that a child was stillborn)

Obtainable from the coroner

Form 100 Notification by the Coroner
(if a death is referred to a coroner but no inquest is held)
Form 101 Order for burial
(if there is an inquest and the deceased is to be buried)
Form E Certificate for cremation
(if there is a post-mortem or inquest and the deceased is to be cremated)
Form 99 Certificate after inquest
Form 104 Removal notice (if the body is to be transported out of England and Wales)

Obtainable from the registrar

Certificate for burial or cremation (if there was no inquest)
Form BD8 Certificate of registration of death
Standard death certificate
Special death certificate
Certificate for certain statutory purposes
Certificate of registration of stillbirth
Certificate of no liability to register (to arrange a funeral in England or Wales when death occurred abroad)

Obtainable from funeral director or crematorium

Form A Application for cremation
Form B Completed by doctor confirming death if body is to be cremated and has not been referred to the coroner
Form C Completed by a second doctor if cremation is planned and the death has been been referred to a coroner
Form F Completed by the doctor connected with the crematorium

Probate forms and related forms

To request forms to release the deceased's National Savings   DNS 904 (SB4)
How to obtain probate – a guide for the applicant acting without a solicitor   PA2
Local offices, addresses and opening times   PA3
Fees payable by a personal applicant   PA4
Probate application form   PA1
Spouses' contributions form   PA5
Statement of stocks and shares etc.   Cap 40
Schedule of real and leasehold/immoveable property   Cap 37B
A return of the whole estate   Cap 44
Application for a certificate under Capital Transfer Tax Act 1984 etc.   Cap 30
Assent or appropriation HM land registry   56
Acknowledging a paid up mortgage   53
Stock transfer form   Con 40
Letter of request   Con 41A
Income tax return form   R59
Income tax deduction certificates   R185 E
Applying for confirmation (Scotland)   Cap A3
Applying for confirmation (Scotland)   Cap B4

Forms from the social security office

Claim for a payment from the social fund towards the cost of a basic funeral   SF200
Industrial death benefit   BI200
Widow's payment claim form   BW1
Guardian's allowance   BG1
Retirement pension claim form   BD8
Invalidity benefit for a widow   SSP 1E or SSP 1T
Application for invalidity benefit for a widow who is not employed   SC 1
Industrial death benefit for certain diseases   PN1A
Family Credit (part of leaflet FC1)   FC1

Useful Addresses

Accept
200 Seagrove Road, London SW6 1RQ (071-381 3155/3156)

Age Concern (England)
Bernard Sunley House, 60 Pitcairn Road, Mitcham, Surrey CR4 3LL (081-640 5431)

Age Concern (Northern Ireland)
128 Great Victoria Street, Belfast BT2 7BG (0232 245729)

Age Concern (Scotland)
33 Castle Street, Edinburgh EH2 3DN (031-225 5000)

Age Concern (Wales)
1 Park Grove, Cardiff, South Glamorgan (0222 371566), (0222 371821)

Al-Anon
61 Great Dover Street, London SE1 4YF (071-403 0988)

Alcohol Concern
305 Grays Inn Road, London WC1X 8QF (071-833 3477)

Alcohol Counselling Service
34 Electric Lane, London SW9 8JT (071-737 3579/3570)

Alcoholics Anonymous (Head Office)
PO Box 1, Stonebow House, Stonebow, York YO1 2NJ (0904 644026)

Anatomy Donations Officer
London Anatomy Office, PO Box 915, London W6 8RP (081-741 2198 during office hours), (071-407 5522 outside office hours)

The British Humanist Association
13 Prince of Wales Terrace, London W8 5PG (071-938 4791)

British Organ Donor Society (BODY)
Balsham, Cambridge CB1 6DL (0223 893636)

The Buddhist Society
58 Eccleston Square, London SW1V 1PH (071-834 5858)

Capital Taxes Office
Minford House, Rockley Road, London W14 ODF (071-603 4622)

Capital Taxes Office
16 Picardy Place, Edinburgh EH1 3NB, (031-556 8511)

Capital Taxes Office
Law Courts Building, Chichester Street, Belfast BT1 3NU (0232 235111)

Citizens Advice Bureau
26 George Square, Edinburgh EH8 9LD

Compassionate Friends
6 Denmark Street, Bristol BS1 5DQ (0272 292778)

The Consumers' Association
14 Buckingham Street, London WC2N 6DS (071-486 5544)

Controller of Stamps (Scotland)
16 Picardy Place, Edinburgh EH1 3NB

The Cremation Society
Woodcut House, Ashford Road, Hollingsbourne, Maidstone, Kent ME17 1XH
(0622 688292)

Cruse
Cruse House, 126 Sheen Road, Richmond, Surrey TW9 1UR (081-940 4818/9047)

Department of Social Services
Leaflets Unit, PO Box 21, Stanmore, Middlesex HA7 1AY

The Foundation for the Study of Infant Deaths
15 Belgrave Square, London SW1X 8PS (071-235 1721)

Gay Bereavement Project
(A telephone service for bereaved homosexuals), (071-837 7324)

General Register Office (England & Wales)
St Catherine's House, 10 Kingsway, London WC2B 6JP (071-242 0262)

General Register Office (Scotland)
New Register House, Edinburgh EH1 3YT (031-556 3952)

General Register Office (Northern Ireland)
Oxford House, 49-55 Chichester Street, Belfast BT1 4HL (0232 235 211)

Health Education Authority
Hamilton House, Mabledon Place, London WC1H 9TX (071-631 0930)

Her Majesty's Commissary Office
16 North Bank Street, Edinburgh EH1 2NJ (031-226 7181)

Her Majesty's Inspector of Anatomy
Portland Court, 160 Great Portland Street, London W1N 5DT (071-872 9302)

Her Majesty's Land Registry
Lincolns Inn Fields, London WC2 (071-405 3488)

Home Office
E Division, Room 205, 50 Queen Anne's Gate, London SW1 9AT (071-213
7006/3044)

The International Stock Exchange (Publications Section)
Old Broad Street, London EC2N 1HP

Hriram Temple (Hindu Temple)
22 King Street, Southall, Middlesex UB2 5AL (081-574 5276)

The Islamic Cultural Centre
146 Park Road, London NW8 7RG (071-724 3363)

The Jewish Joint Burial Society
North Western Reform Synagogue, Alyth Gardens, London NW11 7EN (081-455 8579)

The Keeper
Meadowbank House, London Road, Edinburgh EH8 7AU

London Bereavement Project Group
c/o London Voluntary Service Council, 68 Charlton Street, London NW1 1JR (071-388 0241)

The Marie Curie Memorial Foundation
124 Sloane Street, London SW1X 9BP (071-730 9157)

Medical Schools (outside England)
Aberdeen, 0224 40244 ext 233
Belfast, 0232 29241 ext 2106/2869
Dundee, 0382 23181 ext 547
Edinburgh, 031-667 1011
Glasgow, 041-399 8855 ext 299

The Miscarriage Association
18 Stoneybrook Close, Bretton, Wakefield WF4 4TP (0924 830515)

National Association of Citizens Advice Bureau
115-123 Pentonville Road, London N1 9LZ (071-833 2181)

National Association of Funeral Directors
618 Warwick Road, Solihull, West Midlands B91 1AA (021-711 1343)

National Association of Master Masons
Crown Buildings, High Street, Aylesbury, Buckinghamshire HP20 1SL (0296 434 750)

National Association for Widows
c/o Stafford District Voluntary Service Centre, Chell Road, Stafford ST16 2QA (0785 45465)

The National Savings Bank
Glasgow G58 1SB, (041-649 4555)

The National Secular Society
702 Holloway Road, London N19 3NL (071-272 1266)

National Society for Cancer Relief
The Macmillan Service, Michael Sobell House, 30 Dorset Square, London NW1 6QL (071-402 8125)

Office of Fair Trading
Field House, Bream's Buildings, London EC4A 1PR (071-242 2858)

Oyez Stationery Group (retail shops)
LONDON, 144/146 Fetter Lane London EC4A 1BT (071-405 2847)
49 Bedford Row, London WC1R 4LS (071-242 7132)
105/107 Moorgate, London EC2M 6SL (071-588 1478)
BIRMINGHAM, 55/59 Newhall Street, Birmingham B3 3RF (021-236 1212)
BRADFORD, 9 Charles Street, Bradford BD1 1DZ (0274 722052)
CARDIFF, 31 Charles Street, Cardiff CF1 4EA (0222 224259)
EXETER, Aphinbrook Road, Marsh Barton, Exeter EX22 8DF (0392 33936/7/8)
LEEDS, Enterprise House, 12 St Paul's Street, Leeds LS1 2LE (0532 435491)

LIVERPOOL, Refuge Assurance House, Derby Square, Lord Street, Liverpool L2 1TS (051-709 0144)
MANCHESTER, 28/30 John Dalton Street, Manchester M2 6HR (061-832 5694)
SHEFFIELD, 7 Campo Lane, Sheffield S1 2EF (0742 721508)
Orders are taken by telephone and forms can be sent by post at an extra charge.

Pneumoconiosis, Byssinosis and Miscellaneous Diseases Benefits Branch
Department of Health and Social Services, Norcross, Blackpool FY5 3TA (0253 856123)

Probate
Principal Registry of the Family Division, Probate Department, Somerset House, Strand, London WC2R 1LP (071-936 6983)

Sasine Register
Meadowbank House, London Road, Edinburgh EH8 7AU

St. Christopher's Hospice
Lawrie Park Road, London SE26 (081-778 9252)

Scottish Home and Health Department
St. Andrew's House, Edinburgh EH1 3DE

Scottish Humanist Council
37 Inchmurrin Drive, Kilmarnock, Ayrshire KA3 2JP (0563 26710)

Society for Parents of Children with Cancer (SPOCC)
7 Colebank Road, Hall Green, Birmingham (021-778 2538)

Stillbirth and Neonatal Death Society (SANDS)
Argyle House, 29-31 Euston Road, London NW1 2SD (071-833 2851/2)

United Synagogue (Orthodox)
Woburn House, Upper Woburn Place, London WC1H OE2 (071-387 4300)

War Pensions Branch
Department of Health and Social Security, Norcross, Blackpool FY5 3TA

The War Widows Association of Great Britain
17 The Earls Croft, Coventry CV3 5ES (0203 503298)

Women's Alcohol Centre
254 St Paul's Road, Islington, London N1 2LU (071-226 4581)

Controlling Probate Registries

Principal Registry of the Family Division, Probate Department, Somerset House, Strand, London WC2R 1LP (071-936 7000 Record Keeper), (071-936 6983 Probate Enquiries), Personal Enquiries Room 526
Birmingham District Probate, Registry (Main Registry), 3rd Floor, Cavendish House, Waterloo Street, Birmingham B2 5PS (021-236 6263/4560)
Stoke-on-Trent Sub-Registry, 2nd Floor, Town Hall, Albion Street, Hanley, Stoke-on-Trent ST1 1QL (0782 23736)
Brighton District Probate Registry, (Main Registry), William Street, Brighton BN2 2LG (0273 684071)
Maidstone Sub-Registry, The Law Courts, Barker Road, Maidstone MEL8 8EW (0622 54966)
Bristol District Probate Registry, (Main Registry), The Crescent Centre, Temple Back, Bristol BS1 6EP (0272 273915/24619)

Bodmin Probate Sub-Registry, Market Street, Bodmin, Cornwall PL31 2JW (0208 72279)

Exeter Probate Sub-Registry, Eastgate House, High Street, Exeter, Devon EX4 3JZ (0392 74515)

Ipswich District Probate Registry, (Main Registry), Level 3, Haven House, 17 Lower Brook Street, Ipswich IP4 1DN (0473 53724)

Norwich Probate Sub-Registry, The Law Courts, Bishopgate, Norwich, Norfolk NR3 1UR (0603 761776)

Peterborough Probate Sub-Registry, 55 Westfield Road, Peterborough PE3 6GS (0733 62802)

Leeds District Probate Registry, (Main Registry), 3rd Floor, Coronet House, Queen Street, Leeds LS1 2BA (0532 431505)

Lincoln Probate Sub-Registry, Mill House, Brayford Side North, Lincoln LN1 1YW (0522 23648)

Sheffield Probate Sub-Registry, The Court House, Castle Street, Sheffield S3 8LW (0742 729920)

Liverpool District Probate Registry, (Main Registry), 3rd Floor, India Buildings, Water Street, Liverpool L2 0QR (051-236 8624)

Chester Probate Sub-Registry, 5th Floor, Hamilton House, Hamilton Place, Chester CH1 2DA (0244 45082)

Lancaster Probate Sub-Registry, Mitre House, Church Street, Lancaster LA1 1HE (0524 36625)

The Probate Registry of Wales, (Main Registry), 49 Cardiff Road, Llandaff, Cardiff CF5 2YW (0222 562422)

Bangor Probate Sub-Registry, 1st Floor, Bron Castell, High Street, Bangor LL57 1YS (0248 362410)

Carmarthen Probate Sub-Registry, 14 King Street, Carmarthen, Dyfed (0267 236238)

Gloucester Probate Sub-Registry, 3 Pitt Street, Gloucester GL1 2BJ (0452 22585)

Manchester District Probate Registry, (Main Registry), 9th Floor, Astley House, 23 Quay Street, Manchester M3 4AT (061-834 4319)

Nottingham Probate Sub-Registry, Upper Ground Floor, Lambert House, Talbot Street, Nottingham NG1 5NS (0602 414288)

Newcastle-upon-Tyne District, Probate Registry, (Main Registry), 2nd Floor, Plummer House, Croft Street, Newcastle-upon-Tyne NE1 6ND (091 261 8383)

Carlisle Probate Sub-Registry, 2 Victoria Place, Carlisle CA1 1ER (0228 21751)

Middlesbrough Probate Sub-Registry, 12/16 Woodlands Road, Middlesbrough TS1 3BE (0642 244770)

York Probate Sub-Registry, Duncome Place, York YO1 2EA (0904 624210)

Oxford District Probate Registry, (Main Registry), 10a New Road, Oxford OX1 1LY (0865 241163)

Leicester Probate Sub-Registry, Government Buildings, Newarke Street, Leicester LE1 5SE (0533 546117)

Winchester District Probate Registry, (Main Registry), 4th Floor, Cromwell House, Andover Road, Winchester, Hampshire SO23 7EW (0962 53046/63771)

Index